Alpha I Mis

An Approach on the Background of Instrumental Transcommunication on Planet Earth

By

Sonia Rinaldi

Channeled from Gregory (Spirit)

Copyright

Dedication

I dedicate this work to the inhabitants of Alpha I for their commitment to helping Planet Earth.

Acknowledgements

I WOULD LIKE TO EXPRESS my gratitude towards the friends and volunteers who helped in the completion of this project.

English Edition Editor: Lisa Laniewski

Cover and Illustrations: Amy Zubak and Sonia Rinaldi

Book Design: Amy Zubak

Proofreader: Betty Anne Millar

I offer special gratitude and affection to Fernando, my companion in life for approximately two decades. Today, he lives in Alpha for over ten years, watching over the loved ones he left behind.

Sonia and Fernando Augusto Machado

FINALLY, I EXTEND MY thanks to the tireless Spiritual Friends, in particular Gregory, the spiritual mentor of this work, who has given me the honor of sharing, under his guidance, the Mission proposed by his Superiors.

About the Author

Sonia Rinaldi, MSc, Ph.d

INTERNATIONAL SPEAKER, author and columnist, Dr. Rinaldi has been participating in research on Instrumental Transcommunication (ITC) for over 30 years, obtaining remarkable results in images and voices. As a leading authority in ITC, she has developed new technologies to record extracorporeal consciousness, pioneered the use of computers to record transcontacts, and introduced new devices in the field of trans communication, including telephone, cellular phone, and Skype.

Dr. Rinaldi is Co-founder and Research Director of IPATI – Instituto de Pesquisas Avançadas em Transcomunicação Instrumental (Institute of Advanced Research on Instrumental Transcommunication) in Brazil, www.ipati.org and Rinaldi Institute of Advanced Research in Instrumental Transcommunication, USA, www.rinaldiinstitute.org

She holds an undergraduate degree in Anglo-Germanic languages (Mackenzie University/São Paulo-SP), MsC in Sciences of Religion (Pontifícia Universidade Católica-SP), Doctorat in Sciences of Religion (Pontifícia Universidade Católica-SP). She is fluent in Portuguese, English, and Spanish.

Sonia speaks frequently on spiritual research and has received worldwide media attention for her innovative methods, which have been documented in the 48 books and e-magazines she has authored and published.

Introduction

AN UNAVOIDABLE QUESTION for anyone who has lost a loved one is:

"Does LIFE continue after death?" And, if so, "Is it possible to break through the boundary of these worlds through communication?"

These questions have accompanied Man since his awakening, for there is evidence that our prehistoric ancestors believed in the survival of the soul as evidenced by funeral rituals.

With evolution throughout history, the concept of transcommunication gained a strong ally in the Sciences, especially through the advancement of Electronics.

Superior Plans of Creation, using this resource, began to narrow the link between the world of the "dead" and the physical plane, creating an opening previously overcome only by mediumship.

The advent of instrumental transcommunication arose and started to fulfill this link through devices. This became possible due to these technological advancements, combined with the fact that dogmatic beliefs had begun to show signs of weakness.

Unquestionably, the faith of the man of the twenty-first century is not the same faith that was subjugated centuries ago. Reason tends to grow along with logic and speeds up with the global spread of technology.

Is it possible that Transcommunication could be the way to bring concrete and definitive proof that one lives after death? Time will tell....

But how? Under what circumstances would the leadership that accompanies the evolution of man on Earth give rise to this process?

This is the central theme of this book which was recorded through channeling.

During the 1980's, a Spirit communicator, who introduced himself as Gregory, asked me to meditate for the execution of his mission. I remember that the whole book was written over four Sundays, as he had indicated.

In 1992, I sent the text to Ed. O Clarim, from Matão-SP, who published 10,000 copies - and whose full income was reverted to assist the works of the Spiritist Center Lovers of Poverty of that city.

More than two decades later, I received the direction to resume the same work. In order to reach a much larger audience, we began publishing in virtual format to reach tablets, cell phones and all new media.

The command returned to resume this work in a new way so that what we originally completed would not be lost on the dusty shelves of libraries.

For this opportunity to serve the Spiritual Friends, I can only express my immense gratitude.

~ Sonia Rinaldi

Chapter I
At the Approach Post

———

A COMMITTEE WAITED in the atrium of the approaching platform for the arrival of the ship that would bring the visitors from the distant star among us known as ALDEBARAN.

A slight breeze and a sense of peace enveloped the area, from where the planet Earth could be seen in its blue hues.

The idea of the leader of that spiritual city, Alpha I, was very pertinent to invite visitors who were long-awaited.

The leader, Marcellus, modestly omitted the identity he had carried when he had lived on Earth in his last incarnation. For more than three centuries inhabiting space, thanks to personal credits, he had assumed the supreme role of Advisor.

Alpha I, a gigantic spiritual city located over the central region of Brazil, houses eminent scientists, scholars and researchers who once inhabited our planet. Today, they gather there, continuing their studies and improving theories, with the purpose of supplying future advances for those who, in their later reincarnations on Earth, will bring, in the form of scientific discoveries, new steps for the evolution of mankind.

With advanced resources that we have not yet considered, they are dozens of years ahead of our current sciences. All the evolution that one day will be brought to Earth, we humans owe to these enlightened spirits who, in this exchange, devote their successive lives in search of the improvement of conditions for their fellow men.

Through thermosensitive probes, they capture in their intricate apparatuses constant evaluations as they peer over all that occurs here. Records can occur broadly, encompassing social groups (such as a community), or more particularly (as with the individual).

In addition, there are many control rooms since the condition of the human being is not the only concern of those in that Spiritual City. For example, in one of those rooms, ultrasensitive machines report the ecosystem preservation index, indicating whether the balance of nature remains stable or if there is disharmony caused by forest devastation, water and air pollution, etc.

In another sector, the condition of animals is closely monitored since the inhabitants of Alpha I know that animals are beings in constant evolution. One day, they will be evolved sufficiently to develop reason and inhabit a human body.

But the evaluations of the past decades have pointed, unfortunately, to growing concern.

The human being has evolved indeed, but he has done so by taking dangerous shortcuts. For example, apparatuses from that Spiritual Post have reported that some countries have warlike arsenals capable of the most unthinkable atrocities, and several weeks ago, the Alpha Capture Center reported that a certain terrestrial laboratory had concluded a Machiavellian composition. They discovered a terrible chemical solution, with which they began to produce bombs of very high power, capable of detonating toxic elements that destroy human skin, leaving its victims with huge, open wounds.

An analysis, without any depth, would suffice to attest to the stage of materialism that had spread on Earth, where this divine opportunity called Life, had become, for many, a gratuitous and despicable thing.

The sages of Alpha I concluded that Man had deviated from the way. In other words, he was becoming oblivious to the destiny that the superiors had dictated to him.

The Committee on the waiting platform, in addition to Marcellus, had two more companions of the upper management of that spiritual city and a trainee.

All of them were waiting for visitors from Aldebaran, star of the Constellation of Taurus, where evolution had been known to reach the limits of perfection.

Marcellus hoped that, with the guidance of these more evolved beings, they could find ways to guarantee to Earth a realignment in their evolutionary trajectory.

It was urgent to save this planet, which has received and seen those Spirits who are now watching over it as inhabitants of Alpha, in order to ascend its evolution.

Man had to be saved ... to save the earth.

Chapter II
The Arrival

MARCELLUS'S FIGURE lit up as a gigantic ship materialized in front of the platform.

Hermus, a trainee, was disturbed by the sudden surprise. The leader clarified, "Surely, you were waiting for the plane to slip through our space. It occurs, however, that the Aldebaran brothers have long ceased to use continuous locomotion. They are possessed of knowledge that we, within our current stage, are unable to fathom. They dominate Space and Time. Analyze with me, Hermus, when you were inhabiting the Earth in the form of the incarnate, you lived in a world of three dimensions, correct?"

Hermus confirmed with a nod.

"However, you know that we who live in the spiritual plane today occupy a tetradimenstional space - that is of four dimensions. What happens is that the spiritual atoms deform in proximity to matter, adjusting the ethereal part to the physical mass, limiting the Spirit to a limited world of three dimensions. When freed from the physical body by death, we rescue the tetra-dimensionality. As we evolve, we will enter spaces with more and more dimensions. This is Evolution. One day, through our research, we will gain clarifications which will raise us to other planes and to infinity. However, the conquest we carry out through the sciences will be an inheritance of human beings, because, before we continue our journey, we will have the task of opening to men the path to these discoveries."

Soon the attention of the entourage turned to the passage that opened in the luminous ship. Within it came a spotlight, and behind it came another.

HERMUS, WHO HAD NEVER previously seen beings who did not look like earthlings (since, despite their fluidity, the inhabitants of their city still retained their physical human traits), asked with discretion, "Is that it ...? I mean ... are they?"

Marcellus merely smiled as the two light orbs glided in his direction. The head of the city where the visitors came in closed his eyes, and it was possible to see that he had communicated with the representatives of the distant star. The intense light emanating from the radiant foci changed in the color and frequency of their vibrations. They were actually dialoguing.

Although the small group, except for Marcellus, did not capture the full conversation, the presence of those beings spread in the air an indescribable well-being.

Marcellus's companions had not yet mastered the technique of purely mental communication, but they knew that in higher planes, communication was done exclusively in this way. In a moment, the ship that had served as scenery vanished. Dematerialized.

Hermus, who in his last earthly incarnation been an eminent biologist, was ecstatic. He became even more entranced when Marcellus addressed the group and relayed the "dialogue" they had shared.

"Our brothers in the Universe, with the humility and nobility that characterize them, would appreciate not transmitting their evolutionary degree which, today, makes them resemble small suns. They would prefer to be transfigured into our biotype, that is, to assume our appearance, while recording the need to assimilate our vocabulary. They believe that if they present themselves as similar to us, the inhabitants of Alpha I, they will have free passage without incurring constraints."

He added, directly to Hermus, "Hermus, you be the model. Post here so that our visitors can proceed to copy our structure."

The biologist, who had received several prizes for scientific discoveries from his last passage on Earth (an effort that even earned him entry into Alpha I that advanced post of studies), was now astonished: to be the model for those superior beings who, in their greatness, were not constrained to reduce their level.

Before he could utter a word, two resplendent figures were outlined in space. With human physical traits and the ability to speak, the barrier to the current mental communication "language" of Aldebaran was eliminated, since in Alpha I, only the leader, the masters and the older inhabitants were enabled with instantaneous communication, that is, the ability to communicate mentally.

Satisfied with this new arrangement, Marcellus invited everyone to go to the Processing Center, next to the headquarters of the High Board, and they retreated in that direction.

Chapter III
Genesis and Biogenesis

———

AS THEY GATHERED AROUND the table in front of an immense crystalline panel, the lead advisor of Alpha I made the introductions.

"This is Hermus," said Marcellus, "who disembodied about forty years ago. Today, he is dedicated to training in the Molecular Engineering and Genetics Sector. This is Glaucius, devoted researcher of the ecosystems of planet Earth; in his last incarnation, he was an untiring ecologist who planted the seed of what, in the future, will become a strong worldwide organization in the defense of nature. Here, in Alpha I, he runs the Department of Ecosynthesis. In addition, this is Francis, illustrated scholar, responsible for the Department of Biotechnology. Here, with her group, she supervises the biotic purification of everything that has life but has not yet reached the level of consciousness - that is, from the minerals, through the vegetables, to the irrational animals."

The visitors of Aldebaran raised their right hands, radiating palms of golden light, in a copied gesture of brotherly union with those who had just been introduced. This expression did little to conceal their own evolution, and retreating their hands, they presented themselves with much more simplicity.

"Lunk ..."

"Flênai ..."

These were their names.

Transpiring satisfaction via interstellar communication, Marcellus continued to address the wise masters of Aldebaran by exposing the concerns of those on Alpha I.

"As we have conveyed, a worry has devastated us. We fear for the future of planet Earth, to which, as you know, we care deeply regarding the level of knowledge.

More than once, we have been taken aback by the possibility that political leaders could devastate the world with nuclear explosions. Today, the earth, which seems morally undermined, is equipped, at the mere touch of a button, with a trifling gesture of a single human ... for EVERYTHING to disappear. Billions of years spent by the superiors of creation ... and currently, it is exposed to inconsequential hands."

Looking down, Marcellus went on, "Man has deviated too far from the line that should be the conduit for the fulfillment of his evolution."

Lunk, who for centuries had only used mental communication, found it difficult to express himself verbally, as evidenced by the slowness of his words. He recognized, however that, in Alpha l, few would be at the level of understanding the integrated concepts he meant to convey with the intense use of the mind in all its potentialities.

He slowly stated, "Tell us the history of Earth, so that we may understand the whole of which man is fruit today."

Marcellus smiled at the immediate adaptation of that superior being, operating within the limits of form and word. Concealing his enthusiasm, he asked Hermus to tackle the subject.

Overcoming his initial surprise, the trainee took on the task.

"It started with the origin of the Earth, the planet to which we offer our protection. It originated 4,600,000,000 years ago, as a huge mass of incandescent gases with a very high temperature core. For a billion years, there occurred a gradual evolution that began with the cooling of the crust, which allowed for the formation of the first organic chemical compounds, indispensable for the constitution of living beings. This is how the biogenesis of Earth began, the life that pulsates in the biosphere after billions of years of evolution."

Marcellus, taking advantage of the pause, added, "From that rocky, desolate and previously sterile landscape, primordial living beings originated, of which man is the descendant at its highest evolutionary stage."

"In the search to explain the mystery of life," resumed Hermus, "some incarnated scientists developed research in an attempt to demonstrate the possibility of Spontaneous Generation, spending several decades insisting that rot, or even damp earth, could be capable of producing life. To put an end to this suggestion, one of our scientists of Alpha I reincarnated on Earth, and under the name of Pasteur, demonstrated experimentally throughout his brilliant career the unreality of this hypothesis. Pasteur shared the ideas of Vallisnieri, author of the maxim that says "ALL LIVING BEINGS PROCEED FROM OTHER LIVING BEINGS".

Lunk and Flênai seemed quite engaged with the biologist's explanation which confirmed, once again, the greatness of the "Cosmic Consciousness," or the Whole, which humans call God.

The visitors of Aldebaran, in their superiority, knew the action of the One who propitiates the evolution of each being, spreading opportunities in all corners of the universe.

Lunk corroborated, "There is life in ALL things, but with varying degrees of consciousness."

Marcellus was delighted at the confirmation of the theory he had long researched.

"These thoughts," he said, "which are the basis of ultra-modern physics, have reached Earth very carefully on our part. Yet, one of our brothers, who today is incarnated on Earth under the name of Bob Toben, has been writing an interesting book that will soon be published under the name of Space -Time and Beyond which will advance much of this knowledge. We believe that these ideas will be widely accepted by the evolved minds that govern human science. They will, however, be rejected by others who, with their mental limitations, cannot yet grasp the grandeur and depth of our conclusions."

Hermus resumed his commentary. "When the Earth was cooled approximately 3,600,000,000 years ago, oxygen was not yet abundant, and this favored the formation and conservation of the first compounds that would evolve in biomolecular stages. The beginning of life evolved from increasing levels of organization through information accumulation. At the maximum limit of the inorganic, we reached the minimum level of the organic – known as the VIRUS".

AT THAT MOMENT, FRANCIS delicately interrupted. "We can illustrate the explanation using our holographic screen." The scientific scholar approached a complex apparatus and activated the commands that immediately generated in the vast screen panel a three-dimensional image of the virus. A crystal in the shape of an icosahedron had been carefully delineated.

Hermus continued, "This figure can be interpreted in two ways, attesting that it is the lower limit between what contains life, or the organic, or the upper limit of what does not contain life, or the inorganic.

From the crystallographic point of view, the virus is inanimate; however, if we look at it from the point of view of its activity, it immediately becomes a living being. We call "activity" its ability to set itself on a bacterium and fire its automatic mechanism by injecting DNA into it."

Flênai, with some effort, shared his first verbalization.

"We who study many planets – ours, as well as other, galaxies - see similarities in the power of Creation Cosmic Consciousness which acts through time, in favor of experience, providing that from the INFINITELY SMALL develop SUPERIOR FORMS, able to give support to REASON, WILL and LOVE, which is the maximum lever for the great evolution."

Glaucius, who until then had merely listened, confirmed the visitor's words. "And long was the journey of trials that separated the primordial virus from the current Man."

Showing deep interest, Lunk requested, "Explain to us how this evolution occurred."

"Well," said Hermus, "we should first recall two Laws governing nature. First, THAT IN THE UNIVERSE THERE IS NO LOSS OR CREATION OF ENERGY, ONLY TRANSFORMATION OF AN ENERGY SPECIES IN ANOTHER DURING THE PROCESSES, and second, THAT WITH THE TRANSFORMATION OF ENERGY TO ANOTHER, ENTROPY ARISES, that is, progressive disorder is installed. Thus, the universe, which departed from a gigantic cluster of particles in motion, suffered the action of entropy ... which continued incessantly.

He paused briefly and continued, "When I was personally encamped on Earth, I became interested in this theme of Life. In my role as a biologist, I tried to understand how this could be, as opposed to the natural tendency of everything in the universe, that is, LIFE IS NECENTROPIC. Then, after becoming disincarnate and inhabiting Alpha I, I learned that a colleague, now incarnated on Earth under the name of Prof. Prigogine, will carry forward these ideas. Prigogine, a fellow biologist, felt the need to examine Biology against the fundamental laws of Physics and has been contributing to human knowledge through important theories based on the observations of the functioning of living systems."

Ilya Prigogine: Belgian chemist and physicist, of Russian origin (1917-2003).
His theory of the irreversibility of time is based on the second law of thermody-
namics. He considers that irreversible changes are the fundamental reality of the
structure of the universe. He was a Nobel recipient in chemistry.

HERMUS, TRYING TO DISGUISE the emotion that accompanied his
memories, continued, "However, in spite of the contribution of our colleague,
it was another scientist, who is still on Earth today under the name of Bertalanffy, who added to the subject. He proposed the thesis that the natural laws of
physics do not explain life, unless they are considered "ACCUMULATIONS
OF INFORMATION IN THE GENETIC CODE, PROVIDED WITH
ORGANIZATIONAL LAWS".

Karl Ludwig Von Bertalanffy (1901-1972) was an Austrian biologist known as one of the founders of general systems theory. He proposed that the universe is governed by systems. The same principles govern the different systems - chemical, physical, biological, social, etc. His work originated the earliest research on bionics and artificial intelligence.

RECOGNIZING THAT THE principle of life is similar across the universe, Lunk expressed satisfaction at the conclusions that place the development of science, currently researched in the planetary crust, on the right course for evolution. Very interested, he asked Hermus to continue.

"To illustrate how the scientists deduced this truth, I ask Francis to reproduce the example of the magnet on the screen," said the biologist.

In a moment, a three-dimensional figure of a piece of cardboard was outlined on the crystalline screen. The advanced system of projection of that spiritual city made it possible to demonstrate, in the form of animation, the sequence as, on the square of cardboard, iron filings were deposited at random.

Hermus clarified,

"The emergence of life can be exemplified as the filings of iron on paper - scattered and disorderly. If we allow it to scatter freely, there will be a continuous progression of disruption of the order. However, if we attach a magnet below, the filament will obey the magnetic field and will no longer suffer the possibilities of disorder (entropy)."

Glaucius added,

"A field outside matter is the secret of life. It is true that the seed of the idea that the physical body, independent of life, had already been planted a few centuries ago on Earth by the wisdom of another brother who, in one of his earthly existences, took on the name of Aristotle, a great philosopher. Today, he inhabits Alpha I under the high condition of Master. Many centuries ago, when he taught in Athens, a city on the European continent, he taught his disciples what he called "ANIMA" - the vital principle that moves all living things. Later, the word "anima" was translated and still applies in the earthly vocabulary as SOUL. As you can see, for centuries there has been talk of duality of body and soul."

He paused briefly and went on: "This subject has cut across the centuries, receiving both support and rejection. Philosophical and scientific schools emerged that confirmed this possibility, while others clung to intricate materialism, trying to explain biogenesis through purely physico-chemical phenomena. However, such hypotheses did not find the logic to take root, favoring the convergence of the deductions in the direction proposed by two colleagues, still on the planet, currently using the names of Burr and Northrop.

During the last forty years, both have developed research, reaching the conclusion that EVERY LIVING THING, whatever the species, WILL BE SURROUNDED BY AN ELECTRODYNAMIC FIELD, capable of being detected by means of conventional voltmeters."

He paused briefly before concluding. "For now, let us consider it important that Earth scientists have come to gradually recognize the existence of the FIELDS OF FORCES as nourishers and maintainers of Life. This is the beginning of the path that Science will take to arrive at the conclusion of the inevitable - THE EXISTENCE OF THE SPIRIT.

Then, after assimilating the undeniable biomagnetic field into all that is alive, they will discover that this field is made up of a space-time structure, capable of storing the whole experience of past lives, becoming a historical informational domain."

Francis added, "Scientists on Earth have always faced a challenge. How do we explain EMBRYOGENESIS? How do we explain the phenomenon of RECAPITULATION?" (This is the process by which the embryo reproduces during its development according to the evolution of the species to which the living being belongs.)

"For example, before acquiring the appearance of a human fetus, it RECAPITULATES all of its historical information. Why? Because an informational domain governs the structuring of the fetus!"

Glaucius concluded the explanation. "Here, in our laboratories, we call this ORGANIZING FIELD MATTER that maintains the coordination of life "BOM" – BIOLOGICAL ORGANIZATOR MODEL.

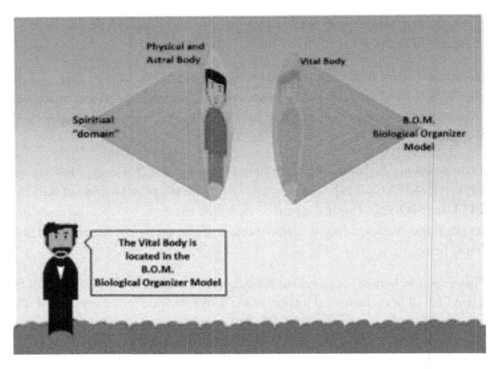

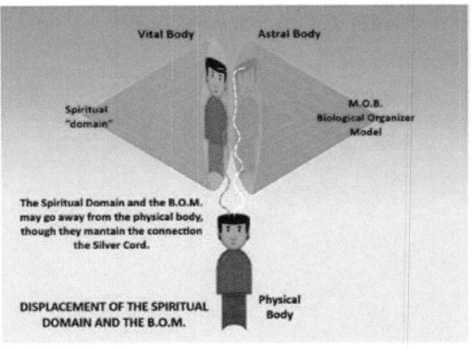

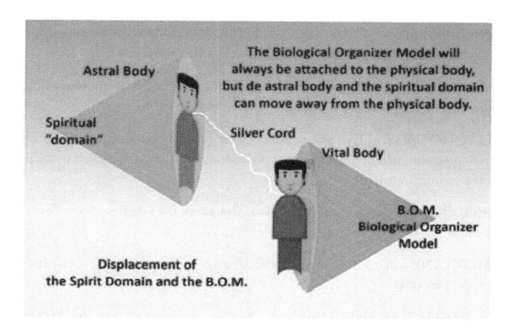

Astral Body

The Biological Organizer Model will always be attached to the physical body, but de astral body and the spiritual domain can move away from the physical body.

Spiritual "domain"

Silver Cord

Vital Body

B.O.M. Biological Organizer Model

Displacement of the Spirit Domain and the B.O.M.

"HAVE THE EARTHLINGS ever discovered such a reality?" asked Flênai.

"Partly." Marcellus clarified. "One of our most esteemed companions, currently incarnated in a major city in the Southern Hemisphere, has been developing steady and secure work in this area. However, protected by deep-rooted modesty, he intermediates us silently. In addition, he has deposited the knowledge he has acquired amongst us in precious books that will someday become the SPIRITUAL LITERACY OF HUMANS.

His theories, which are also ours, do not seem to bear much fruit today. It is still early, and he knows it. For now, he confines himself to developing the seeds and planting them.

The day will come when these ideas will flourish and will be another door for the human being to open, providing new perspectives for the understanding of life."

"In fact, the admission of the existence of the BOM has important applications for terrestrials," commented Lunk.

"Without a doubt, many areas of science will be reviewed in the future. Among them, the concepts of GENETICS and HEREDITY, since the biological and psychological aspects will be observed from another perspective.

The EMBRYOLOGY, mentioned by our doctor, will be better understood, in the sense of the progressive remodeling of the human form.

PSYCHOLOGY will have to consider the reincarnational components of inheritance obtained in previous experiences and determine their levels of influence on human behavior.

BIOLOGY will see, in the congenital deformations, the manifestation of experiences.

MEDICINE will resort to the processes of magnetic donations, acting directly on the perispirit.

PARANORMAL PHENOMENOLOGY will be better understood. Psi faculties will have credit and great applications. The moment is waiting. The planting is being done. The time until harvest will not be long."

The Advisor of Alpha I lowered his eyes, perhaps to remember the figure of that particular friend.

Chapter IV
The Exchange

———

A PLEASANT, MELODIOUS sound, like a soft bell, interrupted the conversation.

Marcellus, using a device similar to a wired intercom, had activated the contact. "Gregory, welcome our apprentices, please, and lead them to the central courtyard where we will collectively pray."

Perceiving the curious expressions of their visitors, he further clarified, "At this hour, we receive visits from the incarnated brothers who inhabit the East of the terrestrial globe. They are Spirits who are attuned to our objectives. We have several shifts of this type of activity to accommodate Earth's time zones.

Here, these brothers are divided into different groups according to their evolutionary stage. Some are INITIATES, who, on Earth, are discovering the truths contained within the various spiritualist religions and are searching beyond these for KNOWLEDGE. Next are the INTERMEDIARIES, the largest group, who are already active in the carnal sphere disseminating the knowledge that they have acquired here. Finally, there are the ADVANCED, who form specialized groups, according to their specific interests, within the wide range of options that Science offers. They are the ones who develop new medicines. They are the ones who are the theorists who create unprecedented scientific theories that help to advance evolution. Everyone here comes, notably, to seek more solidity in their ideas."

Francis, sensing an unsatisfied curiosity, added, "And, because we bring together renowned scientists from all over the world who, having the chance to discuss ideas and plans here, often provoke the phenomenon of almost simultaneous discovery of theories, medicines, vaccines, etc. throughout different points of the world"

With intrigue, Lunk questioned, "But does the terrestrial have a proper space-craft to cross different astral planes, leaving its three-dimensional space for this four-dimensional one?"

Glaucius provided some enlightenment. "Not at all. The science of human astronautics only produces spacecraft to navigate local space, reaching today's apex with supersonic airplanes that travel at the speed of sound and with rockets that have reached the moon. However, there is nothing that would allow them to leave the three-dimensional space".

"But, then, how do they come to this spiritual city?" inquired Lunk.

"Oh yes," said Glaucius. "They arrive by temporary detachment from the body during physical sleep. As you will see in a short time, everyone has a delicate, silver-blue cord attached from the nape of his neck. This thread connects his or her astral body to the physical body the moment they are in deep sleep on Earth."

Francis added, "It is true that, when they awaken, they will not remember with precision everything that they have witnessed here since the physical brain has no means of interpreting this scene's peculiarities. However, what they learn here will be retained in their consciousness and will be exhibited through intuition."

Marcellus spoke, further clarifying this exchange. "In truth, we have several representatives spread across the planet. In general, they are spirits of great moral nobility and high intellectual level who volunteer to contribute - sometimes under even the most difficult conditions. Those who rise to such high degrees, through personal concern for the human race, all deserve great respect from us, and we offer our devotion to each of them."

Flênaí and Lunk indicated that they were impressed by the active work developed in Alpha I, and although they had not questioned, they still had difficulty understanding the general apprehension of that spiritual city in relation to planet Earth

The silence was broken by the invitation of Marcellus, who appealed, "Grant us the honor of your presence at the opening of today's meeting."

In a moment, the high leadership of Alpha I, followed by the illustrious visitors of Aldebaran, filed into the vast inner courtyard where countless human brothers talked animatedly. The curious silver-blue cords that Glaucius had referred to were hanging from each traveler behind the back of the head. The voicing made them aware of their affinity.

As the brothers from Earth registered the presence of the two brilliant visitors, they quieted in rapture, eyes wide, as if they were observing two deities.

Marcellus, who usually opened the study meetings with a prayer, stepped forward and with eyes closed, broke the solemn silence, praying:

"Supreme Lords, the communion of our hearts is the message of thanksgiving for the opportunity that your infinite benevolence gives us.

Allow us to advance, through these brethren who are here seeking the Light of Truth, the seed of Peace to the Earth.

You have entrusted this spiritual community with the protection and guidance of those who live on the planet. Grant, today, that those of us in the position of Masters, also receive from your envoys, our greater brethren, the benefit of the knowledge we do not yet have.

Make us, Lords, the messengers of Your Wisdom"

A short distance away, Flênai and Lunk, in deep concentration, emanated jets of shimmering light from their auras that, upon expansion, gilded the whole environment, transforming it into something that human words could not adequately describe.

Extremely moved by this, Hermus commented to Francis, "Upon awakening at dawn in their physical bodies, our incarnate brethren will think they have visited paradise."

Chapter V
Finally, the Spirit

———

THE PARTY RETURNED to the meeting room to continue the explanations.

It was imperative to enlighten Flênai and Lunk about how Life on Earth began and how it evolved into its highest exemplar - Man.

Flênai repeated his understanding. "You told us that some earthly scholars have already scientifically verified the existence of the BIOMAGNETIC FIELD as a structural function of Life."

"With implications in the BOM - Biological Organization Model," added Lunk.

"Yes," Glaucius confirmed. "The science of the Earth runs up against the confirmation that the human being is not made of pure physical matter, but composed of an energetic field, synonymous with Life.

In fact, Albert Einstein's thesis helped us by proposing a connection between MASS and ENERGY. We conclude that, following Einstein's assertions, even the physical body cannot be considered purely material.

However, progress through scientific evidence is slow, since the five senses of human perception are insufficient to comprehend a wider reality, and the discovery of equipment that would allow humans to expand these limits is linked to a moral evolution that, sadly, has hardly occurred, especially throughout these last decades.

However, what they slowly discover by way of reason, the Supreme Lord allows them to perceive by the heart. Thus, it is that different religions often allow the common man to realize and accept the existence of something beyond matter, something that survives the physical death. This is sometimes called the soul, spirit, vital principle, etc.

The fact is that man, today, seems not to attend to his divine nature. We fear that such disinterest, generated by the materialism that looms over the Earth, will divert our incarnated brothers from the development that best benefits them.

Materialism, that is, attachment to everything that is material, equates to covetousness, which is the sister of envy, mother of authoritarianism, daughter of the thirst for power and selfishness.

This quality makes up the typical reality of the world today.

Materialism itself has always been the tonic of the planet, even by its coarse constitution, that is, by the approach of the spirit to the dense life. However, this characteristic has been growing at rampant levels."

With a wry smile, he added: "Ironically, this grave problem, espoused more widely in the western part of the world, has its origins in the Church itself, whose religion, established centuries ago, prevailed under despotism and fanaticism, involving torture and corruption, characteristic of times like that of the Inquisition, when the church unscrupulously confiscated property and properties that earned it the fortune and economic empire it holds to this day.

It was through the gradual aversion of the plebe against these atrocities that man was compelled to detach himself from religious concepts, valuing reason over doctrine. This erupted at a time later called Enlightenment, with the emergence of Rationalism and Positivism. From there, Man discovered the needlessness of a God that the Church had transformed over the centuries into a tyrant. He perceived that his reason was more and more capable of developing technologies, discovering remedies, curing illnesses, bringing comfort to him and others, giving him the relief that the Church had robbed him of through threats and taxes. This accentuated the scientific progress of the last centuries, since, because of the self-serving interests of the Church, the evolution of Science had all but stagnated. In repudiation of all that had occurred, man gradually turned away from religion. He has become increasingly materialistic in a process that has become dangerously accentuated in recent decades.

In the eastern part of the globe, for example, authoritarian governments have imposed, on certain peoples, the Marxist doctrine, which, in its principles, denies the existence of any superior entity, and religion has been essentially banished from some societies as a malicious plague. In addition, a whole generation grew up under such a line of thought. Thus, while in the East, the origin of materialism could be considered political, in the West, the origin, could be seen as economic. On this other side of the globe, countries that dominate make other people, to the extent that they can, their dependents - generating in the latter the need to safeguard whatever is important to them. This tends to make Man concerned about his survival, wage income, acquisition of goods - in short, everything that suggests a sense of security.

In addition, consumerism spread in all its shades.

We would say that, on this side of the world, those who have a lot struggle to maintain their status, and those who possess little, protest their plight. That is the meaning of world conjugation - everyone wants to have. This is the driving force of the present human reality. Everything else derives as a consequence."

After a few seconds in silence, Lunk asked, "How do you think it is possible to combat materialism?"

Hermus replied, "We have countered with extensive action in an attempt to quell this monster that blinds reason. However, we recognize that our supporters do not struggle with the feelings generated by materialism, such as anguish, etc., alone. In all this we still count on an aggravating. Unfortunately, within the current vibratory pattern that the Man emanates, strong currents of disembodied brothers that inhabit inferior zones next to the crust are attracted by the tuning. This produces a symbiosis such that it demands of us the DOUBLE of Stress."

Interested, Flênai asked, "What kind of action has Alpha I practiced to assist the earthly brethren?"

"We tried to provide them with CONCRETE evidence of the survival of the Spirit," Glaucius said. "On the day they accept this incontestable reality, they will think much more before doing any wrongdoing. We hope that, by acknowledging the inescapability of life after death, Man will return to the path of moral elevation."

"Our mode of action," added Francis, "is always through reason, logic - that is, science - since religions, which by faith touch only the heart, do not reach our target - the materialists.

We have taken our action in this direction, made possible by the exchange of our researchers who, in their successive reincarnations on Earth, gradually escape the obscurity of ignorance.

Although earth science cannot solve and detail the secrets that govern life, numerous researchers have been recording a vast collection of cases that prove, experimentally and scientifically, the existence of something that survives the physical death of the body."

Taking a brief pause, Francis continued, "An example of such experiments are those conducted with the so-called 'Astral Travelers'. These brothers have already developed the ability to consciously detach themselves from the physical body. Thus, although always under the protection of selfless disincarnated benefactors dedicated to this type of training, many are able to leave the physical body while asleep and to go wherever they wish. They visit places or people at night and are later able to narrate, down to fine details, everything they have seen.

This singular type of faculty offers the advantage of enabling laboratory proof. For example, it is possible to isolate the medium in a certain location and ask him to unfold during sleep to a designated place where he should observe and record, in his consciousness, details to be later checked.

A medium of unfoldment, or astral traveler, can improve his abilities and become able to relay minute details of the place he visited – such as giving the hour visualized on a clock at the location, detailing the style or color of the clothes of the people visited, and even repeating topics heard in conversations.

The physical body of the medium, being asleep in its bed, obviously cannot be perceived in the place visited."

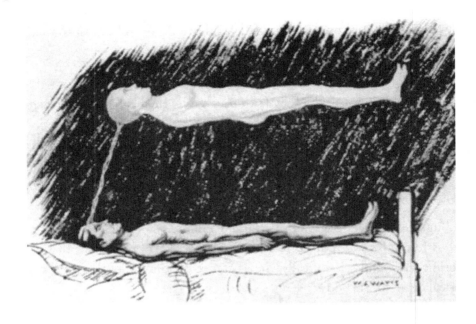

The astral leaves the body during sleep.

LUNK NODDED, AGREEING to the achievement that the knowledge exchange of the brothers of Alpha I and planet Earth had produced.

Hermus, to complement the information shared, recalled his experiences in the area of Biology and Medicine. "Another type of evidence is the testimony of doctors and nurses attending to terminally ill patients. Much literature in this area has been organized by dedicated friends, such as Raymond Moody Jr. In his research, he has highlighted numerous cases of people who, close to the passing of the physical body, describe visions - usually of deceased relatives, with whom they even enter into dialogue. This is the side captured by the doctors; however, what is actually happening with the brothers' physical lives coming to an end is that they are being visited by friendly entities or relatives who come to facilitate the transit of the one who will soon leave the physical body."

Raymond Moody, born in the USA (1944 -...), Ph.D. in philosophy and medi-cine. Forerunner of the research on "life after death", he specialized in the study of the phenomenon of NDE (near-death experience). Breaking with the explana-tions of neuroscience, he stated that it is a phenomenon of a spiritual nature. He has published several books on the theme. "Life After Life" is probably the best known.

HERMUS PAUSED BRIEFLY and continued, "Along the same lines, there are testimonies of people who have gone through the phenomenon coined "near death experiences". These are cases in which clinical death occurs for a few min-utes, but the physical body later returns to life. Treasured records note close similarities among the reporting of people who have experienced these 'NDEs'. This is further evidence that the spirit can maintain consciousness indepen-dently of organic death - that is, the physical body died clinically, but "con-sciousness" or spirit continued to LIVE".

Marcellus then remembered to share about someone who was very special to him. "For the sake of our cause, we sometimes have devoted collaborators - the mediums, who receive this name because they intermediate our (astral) plane with the local (physical) plane.

A notable example is that of a brother still on Earth, but who will return to Alpha around the year 2002, who has been producing precious works through psychography. There, he is known as Chico Xavier. With a high moral standard and high mediumistic development, he allows disincarnated brothers, engaged in high doctrinal tasks, to transmit, mainly through psychography (automatic writing), messages and teachings of inestimable value from and about our spiritual plan.

A close study of the complete works of this great medium will point to the conclusion that undeniably his writings derive from DIFFERENT AUTHORS, and that a single writer could never write such vast literature – totaling 412 books in a variety of styles – if it was not actually the result of spiritual collaboration."

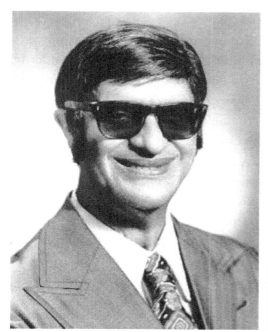

Chico Xavier (1910-2002): Chico Xavier, born in Pedro Leopoldo, Minas Gerais, Brazil, is the most appreciated and well-known medium in Brazil. A spokesman for spiritism, he wrote 461 books, translated into 33 languages. He has sold more than 40 million books in Brazil and throughout the world.

"THIS IS JUST SOME OF the evidence our incarnated brethren have been observing," Glaucius said. "Another form of contact, both solid and eloquent, which points toward evidence of post-mortem survival, is DIRECT MAGNETIC RECORDINGS."

Lunk interrupted with interest. "Direct recordings? How does this occur?"

Glaucius explained, "These occurrences, known as the Electronic Voices, began around the year 1950. The phenomenon was investigated by a few researchers, but at that time, it was deeply studied by Jurgenson, as well as by Raudive, who recorded and analyzed more than seventy thousand sentences recorded on magnetic tapes, which he carefully collected over many years."

"In what way do the recordings take place?" asked Flênai.

"As a brief history, about fifteen years ago our friend, Jurgenson, attempted to capture, unpretentiously, the sound of birds chirping on his tape recorder by leaving his recording apparatus in the window. This was the first opportunity used by our disincarnated brothers to insert the INTERFERENCE ... resulting, to Jurgenson's surprise, in the recording of words. Obviously, he initially thought he had recorded the interference of some nearby radio station, but our disincarnated brothers were insistent, succeeding in improving the way they emitted messages, making them indisputable. A very creative way they used to ensure that such recordings were not the product of radio capture was to send scraps, composing sentences with words from different known languages. It was thus confirmed that it was not a radio broadcast, since none would produce such communication by mixing different languages. It was definitely the result of our plan for Earth's electronic devices."

Flênai, not satisfied, insisted, "How can this interference be handled?"

"Due to the rudimentary stage of the terrestrial recorders, the process is like this: When the apparatus is activated to record, it puts into action a small centralizing focus. This sensitive micro-focus also registers our stimuli, which are the result of our manipulation of vibrations. Since our field of living is mostly ethereal, that is, less dense than the Earth, the energy here enables us to model it with some ease, so as to densify it and make it more compatible with the density of the earth's atmosphere.

When our disincarnated brothers act on terrestrial recorders, they channel the emission of their voices into a refractory tube, with pyramidal geometric shapes inside it, the purpose of which is to intensify the sound vibrations emitted exactly on the said photoelectric cell, making audible voices in the Magnetic tape device."

Friedrich Jürgenson (1903-1987), born in Mülnbo (Sweden), was a painter and film producer. In 1959, while recording nocturnal bird songs, he recorded voices from another dimension. He became a pioneer of Instrumental Transcommunication, publishing several books. One of them, The Telephone to Beyond, was popular in Brazil in the 1970's.

Konstantin Raudive (1909-1974)

Konstantin Raudive was a writer, essayist and Latvian psychologist. After a visit with Jürgenson in the 60's, he also decides to dedicate himself to the recording of paranormal voices. In 1968, he publishes "Inaudible Becomes Audible", where it approaches the 72,000 recordings that would have recorded until then.

LUNK AND FENAI LOOKED at each other with satisfaction. They noted the efforts of the Alpha I brothers in their quest for real contact with the earthly brethren.

From the radiance that surrounded them, it was obvious that they were engaging in dialogue on a mental level. Finally, Lunk spoke. "Great work is what you accomplish in the successful fulfillment of the mission given to this spiritual city. All your endeavors are praiseworthy. We can understand that with this active exchange between Alpha I and the earthly plane, materialism is being defeated. Man has been growing in spirituality, raising his moral level, qualifying for a more promising future. With so much evidence offered to him, whether through Brother Chico Xavier, or via medical testimonies, or through recordings and the study of voice recordings, the earth is finally supplied with evidence of the survival of the postmortem spirit."

Flênai added, "All for the benefit of the human being, for this knowledge will certainly guide them on Earth."

Marcellus was suddenly embarrassed, for although the deduction the visitors made came from logic, it was, unfortunately, far from being true.

Francis, perceiving the embarrassing situation, proposed, "I think maybe we should lead our respected visitors to our home library." Addressing them specifically, she explained, "This department is at the catchment center, where we record everything that occurs on the planet. These records are archived in hyper-rotation holograms - a conquest of ours, in fact, which has not yet been brought to Earth! Here we have perfected in three-dimensions, recording of images under a great reduction of time, so that the entire history of the planet, for example, is contained in a small box of recorded film. It is decoding, so it is not possible at eye level, but at consciousness level. This improvement was necessary, given the volume of data collected continuously over several millennia."

Marcellus concurred, "Doctor, your idea is very good, because it will give our visitors an idea of certain details about the life of our earthly brothers, essential for both of them to approach reality."

"But, even more telling than to KNOW about Man, would be to LIVE as Man. I propose knowledge in loco!" declared Flênai.

Hermus, Glaucius, and Francis looked among themselves uneasily. How would their illustrious visitors inhabit a region as dense as Earth? If they considered the level of an inhabitant of Aldebaran relative to that of a terrestrial, surely they would discover an evolutionary abyss of a few thousand years. Would they not feel embarrassed?

Skilled in mental readings, Lunk and Flênai captured the thoughts of their companions and responded with sweet smiles, "When do we leave?"

Both relief and joy broke out in the countenance of the Alpha I brothers. They recognized that they stood before enlightened representatives of the Almighty.

"Immediately," confirmed Marcellus commanding a smile.

Author's note: In this illustration (which I made myself), I show how I saw at the time the "city" referred to by the communicators.

Friedrich Jürgenson (1903-1987), pioneer of Transcommunication, of the electronic era. The pioneers in the 1960s had only rollers, which gave way to the tape recorder and continued advancing technologically until the 90's when I introduced the use of the computer into the recordings.

DR. KONSTANTIN RAUDIVE, for us of IPATI - Institute of Advanced Research in Instrumental Transcommunication - not only has importance as a pioneer, but for having assumed the Coordination of the South Station that transmits from Alpha I to here. Many years after the publication of this book (Alpha I Mission) we would hear and record numerous references to Alpha as well as hearing directly from Dr. Raudive. He has been with us since the 90s and has become a close friend and faithful collaborator.

Chapter VI
Alpha I

———

WITHOUT THE NEED FOR rest or eating, action in the higher spheres is always continuous.

In Alpha I, where the concept of time is very different from the terrestrial one, there are other habits. Distanced from gross matter, the "bodies" of the inhabitants of Alpha I exhibit an extremely rarefied physical structure, although the visual appearance perfectly resembles that of the human. Of almost translucent texture and very light, they maintain greater density only in the upper region at and above the thorax. They do not possess legs, in the sense we would understand, since they do not need to walk, but simply flutter about.

As they continue to evolve, these ex-humans will lose more and more of these physical characteristics and will become suns, just like the illustrious visitors of Aldebaran. This is the evolution of all. And, it will be ours too, someday.

Being from Aldebaran

MARCELLUS, ORGANIZING their departure, inquired, "Do any of you have vital tasks that would prohibit you from participating in the mission to visit Earth?"

Glaucius and Francis responded affirmatively. Both had urgent obligations on Alpha I that required them to stay at the station. "Then, Hermus, so that we are well prepared, summon Gregory and request the ship DR25. We will meet together on the runway".

Hermus withdrew, leaving his mentor in conversation with the visitors.

"We did an intra-aura analysis," Flênai told Marcellus, "and we find that your level already meets the demands for higher posts. We are considering the possibility of interceding for your transfer to our sphere. Aldebaran, today, would be for you a source of inexhaustible learning."

Marcellus looked up apprehensively and replied quickly. "I am unable but thank you both for your kind consideration."

Lunk thought deeply for a few moments and asked, "Who is the young woman to whom you are bound? Does she live on Earth?"

Marcellus, disconcerted, saw himself as an open book before those superior spirits from whom it seemed impossible to keep secrets. "Yes, she lives," he responded with eyes lowered. "It is the one I chose to be my mother."

Flênai and Lunk contemplated probing further, but it was not necessary since Marcellus stepped forward to explain further. "Several decades ago, I took charge of personally accompanying all of the reincarnations of our scientists and scholars from here to Earth.

I closely follow their evolution there, but, unfortunately, they rarely fulfill the mission to its fullest extent. They are brothers who often live with the honors of geniuses, surrounded by prizes, but are most often impaired by the narrow limits of human logic, rarely recognizing the link between science and spirituality. That is why I am going down to Earth. I am going to reincarnate."

Lunk and Flênai recognized the magnitude of this intention. The Alpha I Advisor had already reached a very high degree of evolution; a reincarnation would now be, by analogy, the same as throwing a lily into the mud.

Acknowledging the silence of the visitors, Marcellus expanded, "I have personally asked the superior hierarchies of our station for the opportunity to try to win this task."

He raised his eyes to stare out the window gazing at the infinite stars and continued, as if dreaming, "The young woman of whom I will be a son is simple, but she is a great collaborator of our harvest. The incarnation will enable me to study the elementary courses of the Earth, such as through universities and other venues, in short, everything that earns me credibility."

Fléinai insisted, "It would be a stifling experience for your current stage of evolution."

"But necessary," Marcellus stated firmly.

Deep in thought, the three of them headed for the docking station where Hermus and Gregory were already waiting for them.

Composing himself, Marcellus made the introduction with a smile. "This is Gregory, our head of the Department of Communications."

The inhabitants of Aldebaran greeted him with special appreciation, perhaps foreseeing something that the others could not grasp.

Lunk asked: "Using the Earth's concept of time, at what point is it in history?"

"The Earth is currently recording the year 1970 AC," Hermus said.

Flênai, radiating more intensely, prophesied with confidence, "Before a third decade is reached, Alpha's priority mission will be fulfilled. Materialism will be overcome by the Science of the Spirit."

Marcellus looked at him with surprise. Suddenly he wished to have the ability to probe inwardly to determine the meaning of that statement.

Hermus, excited by this news, seemed even more energized, and he hurried to lead the visitors into the ship.

When everyone was prepared, the navigator inquired, "Which way, sir?"

"This mission goes to Earth, Andreye, but lead us first to our AC2 verification satellite," Marcellus directed with kindness.

The ship's operator entered the course codes, and in a few moments, the ship silently moved away at high speed. They took flight in the direction of the small luminous sphere, which could only be closely identified as a satellite. They parked and, at the invitation of the leader, disembarked the ship to fully enjoy the sight.

Lunk and Flênai silently took in the magnitude of the scene that was descending further below them, encompassing the whole city of Alpha I, and in the background the terrestrial globe, as if the natural beauty of the universe could somehow feed them. It was the translation of universal union ... or twinning with the observed.

With surprise, Lunk noted, "The shape of Alpha I is that of a five-pointed star?"

"Yes," said Marcellus proudly, adding, "Our city is beautiful, is not it?"

The silence of the visitors confirmed their agreement. "The silver light you see in the center of the star, what does it consist of?" one of them asked.

Gregory was the one who clarified, "The sectoral leaders, who manage from the central summit, communicate with superior hierarchies at dawn and at sunset. What is seen here from this intense light is the communication exchange, as it is happening at the moment."

"We realize that every tip of the star is full of buildings," said Flênai.

"Yes," continued Gregory, "around the dome are the study buildings of the five sectors which unfold all over the city."

"What sectors are you referring to?"

"Well, the five points originate from the headquarters of the central administration, from where the superior designations start. Each sector responds by a source of improvement to be brought to Earth. If we draw a parallel with respect to the earthly cardinal points, we will have the following: To the north are the scholars of the ecosystems; the Eastern tip harbors genetic engineering; Southeast is the biotechnology area; to the Northwest, the advanced students of trans-electronics; and to the Southwest, where we inhabit, the communications teams are stationed."

The visitors were silent as they gazed, appreciating the vision of the homeland of those brothers dedicated to the cause of planet Earth. The presence of the Supreme was felt in everything. Everything shone greatness for the glory of the merger.

Illustration of Spiritual City

In this illustration (which I drew as I was shown) one can see the city referred to by the communicants. Perhaps a spiritual city or perhaps a mother ship located over Brazil.

Chapter VII
Traveling

AFTER THE JOURNEY RESUMED, Hermus informed Marcellus, "The brothers in the specialized clothing area are awaiting us."

"Excellent," replied the Advisor.

Flênai and Lunk did not understand what the ex-biologist had referred to, but they observed that the ship was traveling vertically downward at that moment.

Suddenly they stopped, and Marcellus said, "Whenever we go to Earth, we land at this post, located below Alpha I, which approximates a more acclimatized area in relation to the Earth. This platform has two main purposes - to serve as the basis for putting on guard-clothing for our protection with density as we travel towards the earth's crust and for resting and exchanging of the clothing when we return from Earth to our city."

Flênai and Lunk remained attentive as they awaited further explanation.

Gregory added, "Our structure, which is too thin in relation to the dense matter of the crust, generates extra difficulties for our access and permanence. That is, the higher frequency of our vibrational composition does not fit within the limits of the frequency of the planetary crust, which hampers even our direct communications. In addition, we have to cross fields of intense negative charges, which would make travel extremely exhausting."

At that moment, attendants at that post presented four strange sets of clothes.

"The Protection Cloths, sir," announced the attendant, addressing the Counselor who further clarified for the visitors, "Since Aldebaran's atmosphere is extremely rarified, you would find certain areas of the planet Earth insurmountable and suffocating. This happens due to the characteristics of low vibration and low spirituality. Please kindly wear these suits. When on Earth, you will understand why you need them."

Soon the four travelers were prepared, and the Advisor authorized the departure from the Protection-Cloths station. Crossing the spaces, the journey passed in profound silence, as all of the travelers remained immersed in their thoughts, strengthening their inner desire to contribute to such a noble cause.

When the ship had approached enough to outline the vast continent, the pilot, looking at his passengers, asked, "What is the local route, sir?"

Marcellus advised him, "Our coming to Earth, Andreye, satisfies two intentions: first, to familiarize our noble visitors with regard to our guarded colleagues, that is, our incarnated brethren; second, to present to them some of our researchers, who are currently incarnate in the crust. We should head east. The impact will place them crudely within the current earthly reality."

At low altitude, the ship began to slide parallel to the ground, showcasing a beautiful, although deserted, region. Hermus, observing the sparse vegetation amidst gravel and rocks, commented, "Life fights for evolution, adapts to what is offered to it. This typifies the nature that flows directly from the Order of the Universe".

Marcellus interrupted the brief silence. "Please note below the construction of a nuclear power plant. This region is called Chernobyl and currently houses two of our scientists. We regret that government leaders are misusing the knowledge they have brought from our astral sphere. This plant represents for the world not only the crowning of an advancement in Science, but also a dangerous toy in the hands of children."

"But the handling of nuclear processes, both fusion and fission, requires keen knowledge. Otherwise, it can pose a real threat to the entire human race," Lunk shared with concern. "Are the world authorities not aware of the danger?"

With regret, Marcellus limited himself to the concise response. "They are."

To mitigate the climate generated, Gregory clarified, "Throughout the last decades, two governmental powers have led the world. One, located in the

West, is named the United States, and the other, based in this region of the East, is called Russia. Both have been using Science - and making great progress in various fields - for the benefit of Man.

However, in the struggle for supremacy, both engage blindly, moving in the direction of self-defense and investing their full potential as researchers for this purpose. What matters to each government is to overcome the other, and for this purpose, each orders and demands further scientific production.

No risks or costs matter. They represent the exacerbated feature of the thirst for power. In these times of intense materialism, where the notion of the existence of the spirit is vague, hordes of discarnate brothers of obscurity who roam and attune to human intentions, see in these incarnate leaders their open channel of manifestation.

By way of conclusion, the generic man who inhabits the planet is a plaything in the hands of humans incarnated with disproportionate ambition, reinforced by the brutal force of the army of disincarnated ones who are attuned to these follies."

Hermus supplemented this information. "Through the use of our probes, we have been recording all the actions taken by both rivals. This is how we see that the country called Russia has joined with the small island in the West, called Cuba, and has been flying and transferring very powerful weapons there, which are all pointed at its supposed adversary -the United States. This came to light through costly espionage and has already resulted in a counter-challenge providing a rematch, at a time of great internal problems, starting with racial conflicts."

Flênai further explained, "In the United States, whites do not accept that their brothers, who descend from another ethnicity and have the color of black skin, can share the same environments. There, the white population, with the connivance of the authorities, segregates and attacks the blacks, humiliating them at the level of animals."

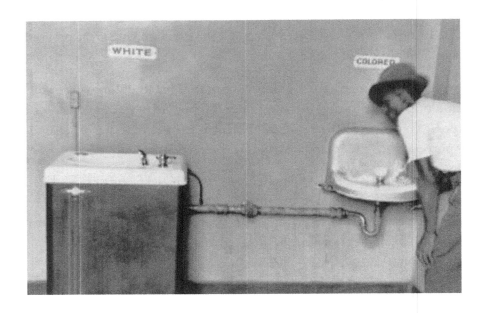

Due to explicit racism, public services were separated with White and Black designations.

Ku Klux Klan - American secret organization of the extreme right, racist, anti-communist, anti-Semite and homophobic, founded in 1865. Preaching the su-

*premacy of the white race, the group was known for its methods of extreme vio-
lence and its macabre executions, especially against the blacks. From the date of
foundation until today, it is estimated that the organization has killed more than
10,000 people.*

LUNK, ASTONISHED, INQUIRED, - "But are not all beings on Earth
there for evolution, regardless of their appearance?"

Marcellus, again, confined himself to the concise answer. "Yes."

Lunk, confused, asked, "In the midst of these illogical actions, can Alpha lay
roots?"

Marcellus reported, "Oh yes, we have many brothers on Earth who strive to sal-
vage the clarity of those who have become blind. On the West side, amongst
the Americans, we had a great collaborator who reincarnated representing our
group of ecosystems. He acted in a remarkable way, even managing to organize
a large demonstration that brought together over one hundred thousand
demonstrators. It was named the MARCH FOR PEACE. The name of this
pacifist, who has already returned to Alpha I, is Martin Luther King, who will
go down in history with the glory of having alerted the world to the need for
balance and peace. A great Spirit, reincarnated in the black race, fulfilled with
gallantry the task that befit him. By his own decision, he had chosen to die by
assassination, so that even more momentum was given to his struggle."

Martin Luther King Jr.

LUNK'S FEATURES BRIGHTENED, temporarily. But soon, dense cloudiness, burdened with a full negative electrical charge, covered the ground below.

Gregory hastened to clarify and, thus, mitigate the shock. "In this eastern region, a great war has been raging for some years now. What we see below is the heavy exhalation of the region called Vietnam."

Marcellus added, "Here, the poor inhabitants are victims of the interests of other nations that seek the local domain. It all began when the Vietnamese wanted to free themselves from the yoke of the nation of which they were a colony. Their dreams of freedom complicated the intentions of the Americans. The United States government decided not to allow the liberation of Vietnam, as this would harm its commerce in the East. And recently, after this poor nation divided itself into two factions, north and south, America saw the feasibility of securing for themselves the chance of penetration in the region through their alliance with the South Vietnamese. Unfortunately, this meaningless struggle has already claimed thousands of lives, as bombings occur over villages, over schools or hospitals, over any place. And the loss is not only of those poor inhabitants, who did nothing worse than be born on that soil."

GREGORY, MOTIVATED by his desire to detail the contribution of his responsibility sector in Alpha I, spoke next. "In order to assuage this heinous act, which may enter into earthly history as the cruelest action of one country over another, in Alpha I we have streamlined our communications area."

With a slight smile of victory, he added, "We have been working with the Americans, who have recently won freedom of the press, and through this achievement, we are making known to the four corners of the world what is truly happening in this region. This has provoked a real uprising of the other nations against the American action in Vietnam.

Janrose Kasmir protesting War in Vietnam in front of Pentagon, 1967; CC BY-SA 4.0

TODAY, THE AMERICAN president, named Nixon, is already under such pressure that he sees no other option but to leave the region."

After a short pause, he added, "At this moment, brothers of our city are acting on Earth, triggering the United Nations Organization, a unit with sufficient power, to influence the decisions of President Nixon to withdraw his troops from Vietnam. We are certain we will achieve this victory."

On the ship, the vision that had been maintained was now hampered by strong, turbid and extremely dense vibrations.

Marcellus, accustomed to expeditions of protection to that region, announced, "We are currently over the hospital of Hanoi. Andreye, let's pause for a few moments." Addressing the visitors, he clarified, "In the vicinity of the bombing camps, the vibrations are less heavy, especially on the improvised hospital here below where innumerable disincarnated brothers give selfless assistance."

"Are these brothers also inhabitants of Alpha I?" Flênai inquired.

"No. Our station is exclusively responsible for the exchange of scholars, brothers who wish to bring some contributions at the level of Science. Let us say that we are in charge of promoting the evolution of the Earth, of giving direction to its course. For maintenance work, at all levels, other spheres of disincarnated brothers take responsibility. They form a broad set of diverse spiritual cities with various purposes. Here, in the region of Vietnam, an immense contingent of disincarnated brothers from different spiritual venues act to aid the injured, wounded, and crippled. Here they unite as companions in this task without respite."

He pondered for several moments before concluding, "We often need the collaboration of these mediators, who act with a lot of practice in consultations and cures, when it is our desire to assist any of our representatives or guardians. Thus, the contact of Alpha I with other spiritual cities is very frequent, since, in the end, the goal is the same - to help the incarnated."

Satisfied with this explanation, but uneasy about what he observed below the ship, Lunk inquired for his own clarification, "So, for economic reasons, a country, foreign to these people, perpetuated this war, transforming that region into an infernal field?"

"Yes," replied Marcellus regretfully. "Outrageous materialism that eclipses the reasoning of the rich American country has made it ignore the depth of descent it has sunken to. However, by Law of Return, America will not go unpunished. Unfortunately, it will pay for this irresponsibility, seeing its children suffer what they have sowed. The American dreams of wealth, glory and power will not last long, and thousands of young soldiers, who have been forced to leave their families, their jobs, their studies, will be, upon their return, the living picture of the mistakes committed – maimed, crazed or addicted to drugs."

Reflecting, he continued, "That's just part of the balance of this irresponsible farce. The death of young Americans is only a part of the package. Despite the efforts of brothers in our plane to aid or recover these soldiers, barely out of adolescence, more than forty thousand of them have perished in these camps. In addition, those who return will never be normal humans again. The drug, heroin, will be the only relief to them, and therefore it will be largely sponsored by its own government, thus creating an irreparable debt to a whole generation of unbalanced individuals."

With an expression of regret, Marcellus continued, "As another inevitable consequence, returning youths will take drug addiction with them and spread this habit in their region of origin. In the near future, the United States will address this internal problem further. Americans will be ashamed of the destruction they have inflicted on this side of the world, as evidenced through the horrors they will be subjected to daily in the coming years, having to live with the crippled, the demented and those addicted to drugs."

They were silent for a moment, until Lunk concluded, "This will delay for many years any advancements for the benefit of man."

"Yes, because the investments made in the war industry are, and will be for a long time, the basic concern of the two governments. It is true that this race, this competition, brings with it a few fruits, for many of our incarnated Alpha I brothers try to carry on with their tasks. In this sense, we see that three years ago Russia put into space a ship that arrived at Venus! This planet is three hundred and twenty million kilometers from Earth! This was a great achievement; in return, last year, the Americans took man to the moon! "Hermus said.

Suddenly, the conversation became choppy as, in the region below them, the intercession of distress was heard. The passengers and crew of the ship listened closely, and soon they detected a message sent by a team of disincarnated brothers, serving as hospital workers below the ship, who mentalized their sphere of origin to ask for reinforcement.

They reported in the message that a violent attack by South Vietnamese / Americans had hit a small rural village of civilians. Six children and seventeen adults, hit by grenades, had arrived at the hospital. The struggle for aid had already begun, and they needed urgent reinforcement. They would send a transport vehicle to those who would not resist and would have to be led to the most distant spiritual spheres, since those in the vicinity were already overcrowded due to the number of dead in the last twenty-four hours.

"We're going to get off," announced Flênai, surprising everyone and filling his fellow passengers with satisfaction. Ground transportation was immediate. When they appeared before the spiritual team that had issued the call for help, they were received like a blessing from the skies.

Flênai commanded reports on the wounded newcomers and went immediately to them, followed by Lunk. The disincarnated brothers allowed them passage, and they would soon see what they could not have imagined.

As they concentrated on the legs of a girl who was groaning desperately, they could see that the splinters of the grenade disappeared and dematerialized. Her cuts closed, and the poor girl, under powerful anesthetic fluids, fell asleep. When she awoke, she would be completely whole.

The dedicated discarnate workers of that service station felt tears of gratitude roll over their faces.

Lunk stood beside an old villager who was writhing in pain because his right foot had been severed. In a state of pity over the man's loss of blood, he fixed for a few seconds upon the stricken region. Turning toward the top of the old man's head, and realizing that the etheric double of the foot had been reconstituted by the old man's own will, he managed within minutes to see the ankle cells multiply rapidly and give shape to a foot that, if not perfect, would at least support it, guaranteeing cessation of the bleeding and the removal of pain.

A Red Cross doctor, a human of high moral standards, had been informed of the new wounded, and his call-to-action was immediate. He took the notebook containing the record of the sick and located the entry information of an elderly person, identified only as being a high-risk patient, due to loss of lower limb and intense hemorrhaging. Finding no one with such specifications, he simply crossed it out, assuming that the mistake was caused by overworking.

He ran his finger across the arrival list in search of serious cases. "Ah ... this one ..." he mumbled to himself. As he looked around the room full of stretchers, he exclaimed softly, "Oh heavens! Where will you be?" He began to walk among those moaning, begging for help, or waiting for medication.

In that short time, Flênai was already beside the pregnant woman, whom the human doctor was now trying to locate. The case was very serious; besides being in a state of advanced pregnancy, the young woman, not more than twenty years of age, was numb in the neck area, which showed numerous lacerations.

Flênai listened as the doctor repeated the woman's symptoms. "Heartbeat too slow, sweating, unconscious, blood pressure lowering".

Placing his right hand on the woman's bleached forehead, Flênai witnessed the events that had transpired on her mental screen. He observed the woman running out of a shack where she had been sheltered when the bombing began in the area. Realizing that a bomb would fall a few meters away from where she had been protected, she started in a desperate race, trying to shelter her belly, turning her back on the shrapnel, barbs and everything that flew through the air following the explosion. She had been struck in the region of the backbone by a large section of the shack that had served as her protection only minutes earlier.

Flênai ceased his observations, for the situation was urgent, and he now knew enough of the origin of the problem. He went on to other investigations. The baby was alive – healthy - but in a traumatic state. He inspected the young woman's spine and located two injuries.

Lunk, who had mentally followed his friend's inquiries, informed Marcellus and the other companions who, in the rear, longed for news. "The girl suffered a fractured vertebral column in two points."

Marcellus felt his eyes moisten, for the conclusion of the diagnosis pointed to the irreversible - the girl would never walk again. As a quadriplegic, she would lie dormant in bed forever.

Flênai, absorbed in his task and oblivious to what was happening around him, declared, "Since we have had our development out of your solar system and never inhabited a human body, we need the intermediation of some of you to maneuver the incarnate physician who, under our control, will provide the material assistance we need to save the baby."

Hermus volunteered. It was only after he had approached the stretcher that he realized that he did not really know how to incorporate the doctor. Although he had never experienced mediumship before, he decided to ignore this fact, realigning the mind for the service to be performed and prepared himself to receive and obey the commands.

Gregory, on the other hand, dominated the subject of communications, and he came together with Hermus to help, instructing, "As I magnetize the doctor, you will try to fit into your upper auric center, assuming the mechanical commands of your hands."

Addressing the more distant brothers, he implored, "Help me in reinforcing magnetization. Our brother, the doctor, is visibly tired, and this will make it easier for him to detach from the physical body, but he is a professional devoted to his duties, and he may be reluctant to yield to his forces. Let us all concentrate so that, under our strong magnetic action, he releases his body, such that Hermus can take over the physical commands."

The order was immediately obeyed, and the incarnate physician, who continued to foolishly attempt to make a diagnosis of the young woman, suddenly found himself losing his strength through sheer exhaustion.

He still mentally forced himself to react, feeling that this was no time to rest, but slowly he began to feel faint, and little by little, his astral vehicle was set free. In a few seconds, Dr. Johnson's double was out of the body.

Confused and frightened, his conscience was troubled. He observed "angels" with sublime features and concluded that he must have died. He was convinced of this as he looked down to see himself acting on a patient with a skill he had never had.

Gregory smiled at the doctor and explained, "We need your physical vehicle to save the baby and, if possible, the mother. Rest your fatigued spirit from this exhausting work that you do here with such dedication and accept our aid for the benefit of these two lives. Allow our brothers to use their physical bodies in this noble mission, which is also yours."

Dr. Johnson spoke not a word and could hardly believe what he saw and heard. However, what did it matter? He felt better than he had ever felt!

He had always believed in the existence of a God/Father who never abandons his children, and, living in the midst of that earthly hell, he became even more attached to his Catholic concepts.

He relaxed his spirit, supported by Gregory, who led him to the ship parked a few meters above the field hospital, a stronghold impervious to the heavy vibrations of the area.

Hermus, tripling his efforts to dominate the dense body of the doctor, suddenly noticed that his mind had lit up. He realized, then, that Lunk, behind him, had acted on his conscience so that he, Hermus, would act on the physical commands of the incarnate physician.

Flênai, who had taken over the general command, found that they needed additional physical assistance. He passed his sensors throughout the lodge and located a nurse with skills for the service.

Communicating from consciousness to consciousness, he made Hermus articulate imperatively through the doctor's mouth, "Christiane, get closer. Let us perform this birth!"

The nurse, surprised and without knowledge of what was happening, exclaimed, "Finally doctor! You've finally learned my name!"

Disregarding her comment and completely focused on the urgency not sensed by the nurse, Dr. Johnson/Hermus ordered, "Prepare and bring the instruments."

The nurse quickly obeyed, already beginning to feel involved through the influence of the disincarnated brothers who had begun to act on her too. With more speed than usual, Christiane streamlined the rudimentary material available. "All set, doctor!"

Hermus, overlapping his hands with Dr. Johnson's physical hands, made himself available to Lunk, who guided the commands from behind. They were three minds immersed in one purpose. They were fused to aid the young woman, whose life now depended on the agility of those hands.

Christiane, realizing that the doctor was about to begin the incisions, asked with wide eyes, "But ... but doctor! Are we not going to anesthetize her?"

Dr. Johnson/Hermus/Lunk did not answer. He had already cut into the ventral region from where, to the nurse's surprise, the woman did not shed a drop of blood.

Flênai, standing at the head, dominated over all the vegetative commands of the young mother so that she did not disincarnate during the surgery. He controlled the pulsations, temperature, pressure, pain and movements.

The operation was swift. Soon, a baby boy was suspended by his little feet in the hands of Dr. Johnson, to the joy of all, while Hermus led the doctor, walking a few steps without the ability that was natural to him, to deposit the newborn in the impromptu basin. Flênai fixed upon the region of the cut, and releasing rays of very high frequency, guided the doctor to close the area without leaving a trace of the surgery.

Christiane, astonished and dumb-struck, obeyed promptly when she heard, "Do not stand there, girl, do your part!"

Lunk and Flênai exchanged information mentally, but it was not made accessible to the other companions. Hermus moved slightly away from Dr. Johnson's body, to whom he was coupled by the mediumistic embodiment, and asked Flênai if the work was finished. "No, we need the land doctor to leverage the mother's body for us. Make him turn the young woman face down."

Hermus straightened again over the dense body of the doctor and ordered, "Christiane, help me to turn the body!"

"But, doctor, she just had Caesarean surgery!"

"Let us turn her around," he insisted, oblivious to the girl's remark.

With the girl turned to the prone position, Dr. Johnson/Hermus moved aside, giving space to Flênai, who began to make the mental inspection, observing the configuration of each vertebra, each fiber, each cell.

He quickly diagnosed, "Tripping with possibility of bone disconnection in the lumbar and dorsal vertebrae."

Marcellus, who was waiting with anticipation, immediately saw his hopes pale. He knew that this diagnosis was likely synonymous with the young woman becoming a quadriplegic forever, that is, incapable of walking, moving her arms or performing any other physical movement. If she survived, she would be relegated to bed.

In the midst of these conjectures, he suddenly felt his hopes revived when he heard Flênai speak. "Lunk, take his vital commands," said Flênai.

Marcellus next saw Flênai, in deep concentration, materialize two golden needles which he delicately implanted into the damaged regions. Fixing strong mentalizations on the needles, Flênai served to channel the energy that was emitted to the fractured point.

Lunk, realizing that his friends did not understand what was happening, clarified, "With these needles materialized in the physical plane, we reinforce the mending power of the subtle energies that in this area of predominantly negative electric charge, could suffer evasion. Through highly potentiated energy, we are doing the micro-reconstitution of the nerve cells, and then we will microfuse the bone cells, based on the model of the etheric double of the ruptured vertebrae."

Marcellus remembered the reconstitution of the old man's severed foot and noted how much this knowledge seemed to be lacking in earthly medicine. This was yet another reason to rush the scientific evidence for the survival of the spirit and the eternity of his individuality in the hope that Man would initiate research on this double of the body, as Flênai now tried the cure.

Momentary anxiety still hovered in the air until the work was completed and Flênai uttered, "Fully reconstituted. Reactivated neurons and integrated vertebrae."

Marcellus, who was observing with an anxious heart, looked up and prayed under the excitement of all, "Supreme Lords, we thank you for the blessing of the opportunity of this work you have entrusted to us. We know ourselves to be mere instruments of Universal Peace and students of your Wisdom. We are eager to be granted the skills to carry out what is of your order. In the name of our incarnate brethren, who through your benevolence have received the help of healing and the chance to continue in the fleshly existence, we thank you and hope to serve you more."

This moment of ingratiation was interrupted only by the arrival of the reinforcement team, requested by the disincarnates of that assistance station, bringing the transport vehicles to those who would die. Astonished, they observed the joy that permeated the environment.

Serious cases had been overcome. In addition, there would be no more disincarnation.

Gregory, authorized to leave, brought forth the spirit of Dr. Johnson and provided his return to the physical body, while Hermus carefully moved away.

Christiane, tenderly cradling the baby who was protected by the few available cloths, informed the doctor, "This is the first baby born in this hospital! In addition, we owe everything to you! No one here had any hope that this mother would make it, because she arrived unconscious and even seemed to have fractured the marrow! However, thanks to you ..."

Dr. Johnson, who had remained totally unconscious during the entire operation, fixed upon the nurse, the baby, and the mother.

A smile crossed his lips as tears clouded his eyes.

Chapter VIII
Still in the East

———

RETURNING TO THE SHIP, the group continued their journey. Despite the satisfaction with the accomplished work, the visitors of Aldebaran interpreted the human condition as very sad.

Flênai commented, "It's hard to conceive that all of this could be caused by the foolishness of a dozen heads making decisions from a distance, oblivious to what is actually happening here. Human versus human ... some acting on others, invading their rights, taking their soil, peace, freedom, life."

Gregory added, "Worse. In this unspeakable action of the Americans against Vietnam, they are not alone. Russia, the other political power we have mentioned, recently invaded a neighboring region, called Czechoslovakia, seizing power by violence. By being militarily superior, they invaded the streets, overthrew the government of the country and seized the rights of the people."

Marcellus explained, "When Man has no beliefs or no religion, he distorts the view of reality, altering it entirely toward himself, as if he was the only living being in the whole universe. He behaves as if all the billions of planets and stars were in the immensity of the firmament only to adorn his vision. In addition, because he only sees through material eyes, he ignores the fact that life continues after physical death, justifying his "right" to usurp the freedom of his fellow man. This is the cold law that rules men today."

Gregory, who had participated through his communications sector in the special work related to the subject, reported, "Yes, but history will have to suffer reversal. In this region of great aridity of faith, called Russia, we have already taken care to embody one of our eminent philosophers, whose role will be to become leader of the Soviets and reverse the direction that now exists.'

He paused briefly and concluded, "If our commander agrees, we could visit him, since we are nearby."

"Excellent, Gregory," replied Marcellus, "It will undoubtedly be a great opportunity to introduce one of our illustrious Alpha I brothers serving on a charitable mission on the planet."

Addressing the pilot, he instructed, "Andreye, lead us to the residence of Mikhail."

"Yes sir!"

The ship flew back westward, crossing cities that, at that moment, began to turn on the lights. It was dawning in Stavropol, near Moscow. Over the city, the ship lowered and finally parked. "Let's all go down."

The group entered Mikhail's house and found him already awake. Gorbachev, thirty-nine, his face tense, did not hide the apprehension he carried within himself. The visitors probed him.

Marcellus, touching his shoulder affectionately, acknowledged, "We have placed much hope in this man for the political restructuring that the East requires today. He is currently Secretary General of the Party but is moving to the top position to try to change the history of this Union of Soviet Socialist Republics. Here, the domain is repressive, and life is appalling. Mikhail, moved by a superior nature and courageous ideas, will promote profound changes, which will be a great milestone in the history of this Union. However, this is a thing of the future."

Under the blessings of the invisible benefactors, Mikhail suddenly felt indescribable well-being. Smiling, Marcellus suggested that the party withdraw.

Mikhail Gorbachev

Editor's note: When this book was written (channeled) in 1985 no one was thinking of the importance that M. Gorbachev would have for Universal History. Years later (1991), under his command still, the USSR (Union of Soviet Socialist Republics) undoes itself, propitiating the independence of the countries that composed it.

Chapter IX
Returning

———

AS THE SHIP ROSE AND began to accelerate, Lunk inquired, interestedly, "You have reported that the terrestrials have already taken a trip off their planet and you even said that it was an achievement by one of the two political powers whose aim was to show their superiority."

"Yes, about a year ago, when calendars marked the year 1969, man came to the moon," Marcellus said. "Regarding the accounting of time used by the incarnates, it is good to clarify that it is marked by the translation and rotation of the Earth in relation to the Sun - what they refer to as a 'day'. When the satellite Moon completes one turn around the Earth, they call this a 'month'; and a complete turn of the planet around the Sun is called a 'year'. Currently, they register the year of 1970."

"A year of global turmoil," stammered Hermus.

"The arrival of Man on the Moon was possible thanks to the presence on Earth of some of our collaborators who, before reincarnating, took on the task of bringing to the planet several of their researches developed in Alpha 1."

Buzz Aldrin salutes the U.S flag on the Moon

BEFORE LUNK OR FLÊNAI demonstrated satisfaction with this "success", Marcellus clarified, "But not always do those who arrive here in a carnal vehicle correctly fulfill the mission assumed. A case that exemplifies this is that of one of our physicists, who here on Earth was called Wernher Von Braun, incarnated in Germany and entrusted with a precious mission. However, he became disillusioned by the situation occurring in his country and emigrated to, and served in, the United States, making his noble knowledge true inversion in his career. Von Braun was the inventor of the V1 and V2 bombs, blockbuster, long-range missiles, and other devices that cost him his transfer from Alpha I to a lower sphere. It is true that Von Braun received much coercion, much seduction in the terrestrial plane, but nothing for us justifies his unspeakable actions."

Wernher Von Braun was the leading figure in the development of rocket technology in Nazi Germany and later a pioneer of rocket technology in the U.S. Inventor of long-range missiles V1 and V2

FLÊNAI, PERCEIVING the embarrassment of Marcellus, resumed, "About the trip to the moon ..."

"APOLLO 11's trip took Man to cross three hundred and eighty-four thousand kilometers of space, lasting four days between launch and landing. This fascinating enterprise of the Americans cost the nation countless millions of dollars, far more than it would take to quell the hunger of the African brothers who are now consumed in Ethiopia in cruel misery, dying by the hundreds every day."

Hermus, somewhat critical, added, "One of the three astronauts who undertook this journey, and who first stepped on the lunar soil, said, as has been captured by thousands of television sets all over the planet, 'This is a small step for man, but a great step for humanity' ..."

Laughing, he concluded, "We others are sure that this is not exactly true, be-cause this euphoria will cease, and for some decades this project will be aban-doned. Therefore, we can say that this was another venture synonymous with American megalomania, trying to go beyond its limits, but that by designation of our superiors will not continue, at least in the coming decades.

Hermus, perhaps sensitized by reality, lost some of the peculiar superiority he possessed as an inhabitant of Alpha I to more resemble his former personality when incarnated, allowing a certain irony to underlie his statement,

"Man will soon realize that an event such as that which occurred in 1492 - when the Europeans discovered America - was MUCH more significant in terms of earthly history than this mighty enterprise of the Americans which, among oth-er reasons, was also likely accomplished to divert attention from the horrors they practiced in Vietnam. If these material resources had been diverted to re-search, for example, in the medical field, surely they would have found medi-cines and cures for diseases whose causes still defy human knowledge."

After a pause, Gregory said thoughtfully, "When we entered this adventure, others registered intentions, beyond research and scientific advancement, that obviously were not divulged. Besides showing their superiority towards the Russians and diverting the attention of the various countries to the atrocities committed in Vietnam, they had another objective - to make the Moon a strate-gic point of war."

Lunk attested, "Apparently, greed is peaking in some of the terrestrials."

"Yes," Gregory agreed, "but Man in general picks up the error in his uncon-scious. That is why a generation today rises up against these armaments, and it will be the hippy community, the seed that will effectively act to change the ma-terialistic course in which the incarnates are mired."

Marcellus explained further, "These young people, who today question the va-lidity of nuclear power plants, the construction of the atomic bomb, and the need for 'money or material goods', defy all the concepts established by the pre-vious generation. These young brothers came in masse from astral spheres and who, according to the designs of our Glaucius honorable responsible for the ecosystem balance, offered for this contribution to Earth. We believe that this seed of hippie irreverence will cause many of the human VALUES to be reconsidered. They bring with them a devotion to nature, care of the globe with natural foods and the detachment of everything that is material. With this, they will be bringing the Man back to Earth... that is, taking back his interest that arrived at the distant Moon, back to his simple day to day life. This is another victory for Glaucius and his dedicated team."

Lunk, still trying to absorb the human view of life, asked, "Do you believe that Man would attempt brutal domination over other forms of life if he located them outside his planet?"

Hermus, with a sad expression, said, "No doubt. Several ground laboratories are developing studies on the likely description of the atmosphere on neighboring planets in an attempt to locate life. Man believes himself to be the center of the universe and that everything else exists for his use and benefit."

"Fortunately, he ignores that within his solar system, composed of planets among which the Earth is one, biological life forms rehearse their evolution, but they do so outside of human access. And more than that – he ignores that OTHER FORMS of 'life' exist on the Earth itself, without his being able to capture them."

"Clarify," implored Flênai.

Hermus continued, "You see, we are non-biological ways of life, but we have our individuality. Like Alpha I, innumerable other cities surround the planet Earth, being located more or less close to the crust, according to its evolutionary stage or need of its services. And all this is inaccessible to Man."

Taking a brief pause, he felt that it was still not clear. He elaborated, "It is that Man inhabits a three-dimensional space, while we, disembodied, inhabit the contiguous space, that is, TETRADIMENSIONAL."

Flênai questioned, "Man recognizes this limit?"

"Not yet," answered Hermus, "but human Science has shown him his littleness in terms of perception, attesting that much is beyond his grasp."

"For example," added Marcellus, "devices constructed here prove that the human VISUAL FIELD begins with red, at three hundred and forty-five trillion cycles per second, and comprises the small scale of light to violet, with seven hundred and fifty trillion cycles per second. Man, however, knows that beneath the red there is not only the infrared, but also countless other waves that are unfathomable to him, and that besides the lilac there is the ultraviolet, which his eyes do not capture, and everything beyond, even if it is thought to him."

Pausing, he continued, "The same is true of SOUND. That is, human hearing comprises a small scale of range, beginning with the sixteen cycles of bass sounds up to one hundred and forty thousand trebles. However, through apparatus that amplifies the capturing capacity, Man knows that below the serious sound are the infrasounds, the radio waves, etc., and besides the treble are the ultrasounds and others, which, for his ears, are inaudible. That is, he begins to observe that he is a limited being."

Limits of human perception

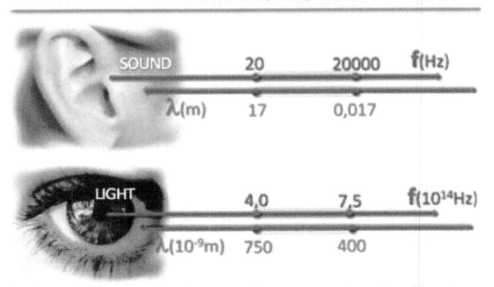

MARCELLUS, PERCEIVING the interest of the visitors with regard to the point of view of the incarnates, directed the pilot of the ship, "Andreye, let's go to South America. We have something special to show our visitors there."

Seeing himself at once answered, he clarified: "With respect to the limits of human understanding, one already faces the barriers of the third dimension, since his understanding, in relation to certain phenomena, already leads him to intuit on another space....what exists in the fourth dimension? In addition, if he continues in logic, he will deduce about greater realities, such as the existence of the fifth, where our noble visitors dwell, and others that still inaccessible to us."

Lunk, showing interest, asked, "Can you capture parallel realities?"

"Through faith, a long time ago. However, experimentally, only more recently have they developed research in the field. Because these are works of our competence, we are directly involved in these surveys, whose example we can share soon. We will visit a center of terrestrial research on paranormal phenomena, installed in the city of São Paulo, where we are headed now."

Lunk and Flênai expressed satisfaction with the conversation. One of them questioned, "How are they inferring about the existence of a space other than the three-dimensional where they live?"

"Through some doctrines, the bond or communication is favored among the disincarnated, as we are, and the incarnates that dwell therein. In these communications, there are some types of manifestation by brothers in our plan, always with the use of mediums - who foster interchange through incorporation, psychophony, psychography, clairvoyance, psychokinesis, telepathy, etc., as well as other manifestations that depend less on the performance of our plan and more on the individual evolution of these mediumistic brothers, such as astral voyagers, seers, mediums of physical effects, etc."

"However, this form of interaction of both spaces (material and spiritual), however obvious it may be, is still regarded as subjective and therefore not accepted by the scientific community, from whom we seek the endorsement."

Flênai, not understanding this need, asked, "Because...?"

"Because we believe that at the moment when Man is obliged to conscientiously accept, in an irrefutable way, the reality of the existence of life after earthly death, much will change, and it is the desire to effect this change that guides us today," stated Marcellus.

Lunk asked for details of what he was doing to prove the existence of another dimension.

Marcellus clarified, "It was said by one of our scientists, currently residing in New York, named H. Shaphey something like the following: WITH EXPRESS AND CURRENT NEURALHUMAN EQUIPMENT, WE ARE NOT APPROPRIATE TO KNOW EVERYTHING FOR THE PURPOSE OF ANYTHING; THERE ARE COGNOSIBLE FIELDS THAT WE DO NOT EVEN UNDERSTAND BETTER TO CONCLUDE THAT WE IGNORE THEM."

The companions laughed at the truth of this statement.

"With regard to the universe, Man already deduces that it is dynamic, is in expansion and has form that implies in the curvature of the cosmic space. In addition, this space is made up of a spatial multiplicity. Physics today strives to understand the intimacy of matter and, with it, define its reality. To attend to the rationalism of eminent researchers, we have caused phenomena to occur that, under strict control of respected observers, enable science to judge its truth."

Flênai made a signal for him to go on.

"The phenomena known as POLTERGEIST are evidences that we, intangible and intelligent beings, can act physically on three-dimensional matter. This is a type of paranormal phenomenon which, as a whole, such as spontaneous combustion, apports etc., already awakens the scientific community for investigations."

Poltergeist Occurrences

AT THAT MOMENT, THE ship already reduced its height in relation to the Earth, and a gigantic city was observable.

"We fly over a large capital, where millions of people now live. They live at an intense pace, consumed by the economic interests that plague the globe today. However, we have planted one of our strongholds here. We will shortly visit the Brazilian Institute of Psycho-Biophysical Research, led by one of our most beloved representatives of Alpha l on Earth. Under his guidance, a team of researchers of paranormal phenomena takes care of records with scientific precision."

The ship parked, and from it could be seen the vibrating effervescence of the big city and the splendor of the moon in the west, beautifying the scenery.

There, Man had taken the first step that he judged to be great ... of a journey that, for a long time, will not continue.

Dr. Hernani Guimarães Andrade, founded the IBPP - Brazilian Institute of Psycho-Biophysical Researches in São Paulo - SP, and was the one who leveraged the scientific researches of spiritualistic themes in that country.

Chapter X
From Another Dimension

Author's Note: The Brazilian Institute of Psychobiophysical Research was on the 3rd floor of this small building in São Paulo. Since the Institute was formed, it was supplied protection in a cylinder format so that all other-dimension aircraft could perceive that it was a safeguarded place. Many large cities have dense vibration, and the purpose of the cylinder is to isolate it from the surrounding vibrations. Many Spiritist centers are afforded this protection, though some are in the form of a bubble, which is for receiving local Earth visitors. The cylinder format is for visitors from outside of Earth. Above the physical building is a much larger spiritualist building that cannot be perceived from the third-dimension view. This is where spirits attend to learn about the research being made by the Institute.

AS THEY DISEMBARKED the ship, the inhabitants of Aldebaran noted, with surprise, that they descended inside a translucent cylinder.

Marcellus, realizing their bewilderment, explained, "Every densely populated city, like this capital, weaves upon itself, with emanations of the vibrations of its human mass, a true network - almost smoke-filled - sufficiently cohesive to attract and feed low-brethren, who here find shelter for their present evolutionary stage. The cities by the sea are always more pleasant for the residents themselves - among other reasons, for the easy dissipation of energy that does not condense over the city, facilitated by evasion towards the sea."

He paused to point the way for the entourage to follow to the insulation panel, cylindrical in shape and whose transparency allowed clear inspection of the city.

Marcellus continued, "These megalopolises, because of their immense size, are always areas of extremeness - large numbers of poor, large numbers of beggars, large numbers of homicide occurrences, countless accidents and so on. For this reason, since the guidance of this Research Center based in São Paulo founded it, in the 1950s, protection was provided to us in the form of the cylinder that you now observe."

Pointing upward, he concluded, "We enter via the landing center, easily identifiable by the friendly ships, and we isolate ourselves from all the vibratory interference of the area."

Hermus further clarified, "Many Spiritist centers have similar protection. Most are only in the form of BUBBLES, since they receive, in general, local visits. Others, who proceed from a greater distance - and are more unaccustomed to the density of the crust - often carry delicate equipment and more commonly travel in ships, although by wearing the clothes guards, we could also travel to Earth without any vehicles."

Marcellus, pleased with the clarification, suggested that they descend the cylinder.

This Institute, located on the third floor of a small building, would never give its incarnated visitors a full appreciation of the immense area that it sheltered on a spiritual level.

Entering the Headquarters, Marcellus' entourage was able to observe a team of researchers incarnated in active work. Flênai approached a young woman who was transcribing the lines of a tape recorder onto paper.

"This is a great collaborator of ours. She is making annotations about a curious case the group is researching, a phenomenon of POLTERGEIST," informed Hermus.

"I understand that studies of phenomena conclude on the 4th Dimension," stated Flênai.

"Yes, here they make studies of sciences, mainly of Physics, in which the attending team tries to find coherence for the paranormal phenomena that they investigate. Recently, they studied the Theory of Relativity and Quantum Mechanics, where they absorbed advanced concepts of Science. During these sessions of study, we always make present some of our instructors, to guarantee the clarifications that are necessary."

He paused and added, "The leader of the Institute, besides the knowledge acquired before the present incarnation brought from Alpha I, is also favored because of his inquisitive mind. A few years ago, he had read about the experiences of Johan Zöllner, carried out in the year 1877 - almost a century ago."

Johann Karl Friedrich Zöllner

LUNK ACKNOWLEDGED THE pause, and not wishing for the subject to deviate, asked for more clarification.

"Professor Zöllner, along with renowned German scientists, has developed valuable research working with the medium, Slade, in the city of Leipzig."

Gregory added, "We, at the time, took care to make the issue of "INTRIGU-ING KNOTS" as they were called, known through the European press."

Hermus explained, "Zöllner and his investigators began their investigations to observe paranormal phenomena using ropes. During the first experiment, the professor took a piece of rope and tied the two ends together. On the amendment, he placed a strong seal which created an inviolable circle. Then, holding the seal between his thumbs, and before respectable witnesses, he sat down before the medium, Slade, who remained seated with both hands on the table all the time. Within moments, everyone was surprised to see that the rope now had four knots!"

Flênai, possibly accustomed to all possibilities of spatial interplanar interference, smiled and asked, "And did they realize that such an effect was produced by the action of agents external to the three-dimensional space they inhabit?"

"Ah yes. Zöllner provided some alternative explanations in response. The one that most satisfied him was the most obvious - that it was about the existence of a four-dimensional hyperspace, from where its inhabitants are capable of operating within a three-dimensional space," Marcellus said.

"The scholar also found what they call APPORTS, that is, the disappearance and reappearance of objects," said Gregory, pointing to two books on the IBPP shelf. "In this compendium called Transcendental Physics and in this other, Scientific Evidence of Survival, Zöllner made a valuable contribution to human culture."

Lunk was interested. "And what was the receptivity of these phenomena?"

Hermus, smiling, said, "For the lay public, or for the victims of the phenomena of POLTERGEIST, it was usually received with much apprehension. Those interested in studying the phenomena further, with the discovery of some case ran to start the research. Opinions in the scientific environment are still divided. Zöllner was adept at explaining that, in APPORT phenomena, for example, solid objects cross three-dimensional space into the four-dimensional space, and finally return to the three-dimensional space. Another researcher, named Ernesto Bozzano, provided another explanation. He suggested that the objects are DEMATERIALIZED and thus disaggregated through the molecular interstices of material barriers, that is, the transposition of matter through matter."

Ernesto Bozzano

FLÊNAI INTERRUPTED, "But both phenomena are possible. One does not exclude the other, and all require spiritual agents."

Marcellus approached the researcher who bent over countless books and commented, "Without a doubt, even the case that our sister is studying includes curious occurrences of APPORTS."

"A few months ago," Hermus explained, "the IBPP team learned of a phenomenon of POLTERGEIST that has been taking place in a nearby city called Suzano. Since then, the group has made several inroads to the place, from where they bring all these films, photos, recordings and endless notes as a result of their interviews. This is the scientific method of presenting a case, so that there is no doubt as to its truthfulness."

"The phenomena of POLTERGEIST, usually, cause certain noises wherever they occur and frighten some people. The word derives from the German words 'poltern' which means 'to make noise' and 'geist' which translates to 'spirit' - that is, originally the name indicated 'noisy spirit.'"

"If these lower brethren only made noise, that would be great. The fact is that they also tend to cause several other phenomena, such as PARAPYROGENIA, that is, spontaneous combustion; APPORTS, such as the sudden disappearance or reappearance of objects, and they often cause BREAKAGE of glasses or dishes. They have even been known to throw stones and promote physical aggression. With this, they often frighten people, provoking great disharmony where they act."

"This is the negative side of these phenomena," Gregory interpreted. "On the other hand, because of the display they create, they call attention to themselves and may be the focus of studies that result in evidence of our existence, the incorporeal, four-dimensional beings acting on the three-dimensional space."

Marcellus continued, "There are innumerable records of respectable researchers with regard to APPORTS cases. As for the scientific interpretation, the one closest to reality is the one of the Frenchman R. Sudre (15), that in the work called "The New Enigmas of the Universe" says more or less the following, among other important topics: now that Einstein didn't hesitate to deform Space and Time to explain the great natural forces, nothing is more possible than to add a fourth dimension to space to explain, for example, the miracle of telergy and make KNOTS on a rope without free ends."

Flênai was interested in becoming more acquainted with the research stage of the phenomena of POLTERGEIST on Earth, to which Gregory alluded, "One of the greatest researchers of the subject was Émile Tizané, who cataloged a large number of cases, especially in France. These phenomena, as was said by the well-known philosopher Allan Kardec, occur by the action of low-level spirits with various intentions. Sometimes, they simply wish to amuse themselves; others desire to do evil to those they bother, or even do so at the command of someone else (for example, magic works or yard, etc.)."

He paused briefly and continued, "For such phenomena to occur, the disincarnated brothers invariably need the help of an incarnate, resident in the place, who, scientifically, receives the name epicenter. As for the duration, phenomena sometimes last a few hours, several weeks, or even years of activity!"

"The one that has been studied here at the Institute has been continuing for about two years. It has been a period of torture for the residents of the house who suffer this harassment," commented Hermus.

Marcellus, acknowledging the interest of the visitors at the mentioned phenomena that evidence the non-physical reality, suggested, "I think that a clearer understanding can be obtained by a visit to the place 'INFESTAD', as it is called, the place of occurrences."

Lunk accepted the suggestion well, and before he left the IBPP and headed toward the ship, he looked upward in concentration, and obtained luminous particles of pleasant perfume and silver-gold in response. It was his blessing to the dedicated IBPP workers in favor of "a parallel Reality".

Albert Einstein

Allan Kardec

Emile Tizané

Chapter XI
The Poltergeist of Suzano

———

AS THEY TRAVELED, GREGORY reviewed the history of the case to be highlighted.

"In the year 1964, that is, six years ago, the bricklayer Jeziel Eleutério de Souza, married to Dona Ana Maria da Conceição, had an affair with Cristina da Silva. He later abandoned his wife and three children to go live with his lover.

Ana Maria suddenly found herself in the position of having to work long hours as a seamstress in a factory, forcing her to pass on the burden of housework to her nine-year-old daughter, Laura. As a result, the young girl had to interrupt her studies. This child, Laura, will later become the "epicenter" of the phenomenon. After four years, Mr. Jeziel returned to his marital home, after separating from his former lover. Cristina, seeing herself deprived of his affections, promised diabolical actions in return."

Gregory paused briefly and continued, "Following her father's return, Laura was agitated and became an unhappy and aggressive teenager. The first phenomena of POLTERGEIST can be traced back to approximately this time when the small house where they lived became the target of stones that were mysteriously thrown at it.

These occurrences were unpredictable and happened both day and night. However, for about the last six months, the situation has undergone an unexpected resurgence. The spiritual attackers have begun to break roof tiles and windows and to throw heavier objects, such as bricks, whose impacts are causing more damages.

Recently, the team of IBPP (Brazilian Institute of Psycho-Biophysical Research) was in the area and counted no less than a hundred and seventy-six broken tiles, which in itself reveals the violence and intensity of the phenomenon.

In May of this year, 1970, this team obtained factual records of parapirogeny occurring at the location. One of the first spontaneous combustions occurred in the bedroom of the couple, when their mattress began to catch fire. Since they arrived in time to prevent everything from burning, they reserved the clothing that was unaffected by the fire, bundled it together, and, transported the bundle to the yard. A little more than an hour later, the clothing smelled burned. The smoke coming from inside the wrapped bundle had detected the combustion! Other phenomena have happened, but the most frequent and dangerous are those of combustion."

Flênai interrupted, "Besides the IBPP members, have these occurrences been observed by others?"

"Yes, of course," replied Hermus. "Even by the police! We recently met the regional delegate, Dr. João Lázaro Rodrigues, together with his police technician, Mr. Natal Samuel de Lima. Following their reports, this case was publicized in the press all over the country."

Poltergeist Attack

*Parapirogeny - Appearance of the partition board of a wardrobe. This is sponta-
neous paranormal combustion during the Suzano Poltergeist (SP-1968/1970).
In this Poltergeist 17, outbreaks of spontaneous combustion were reported.*

THE SHIP FINALLY PARKED in a poor, arid region, which emanated a certain morbidity in the air.

"Again, we need to use clothes-guards. This area is similar to the heavy area we
visited hours ago in the Vietnamese region and would be unsustainable for us
without guards.

Spirits who often work near the crust do not wear any kind of special clothing,
but clothes such as the ones we wear have already been observed on Earth even
in the distant past. A book was published under the title Were the Gods Astronauts? in which the author reveals the many apparitions of beings that bor-
dered on what was considered 'strange garments.'"

"The fact is that if we were to leave the ship in this region of low vibration without protection, our auric centers would suffer disorder caused by the amassed

loads that would roar over us like iron filings on magnets," Marcellus said. "Let's go down and see the phenomena that have intrigued this entire neighborhood."

Given the high spiritual standard of the entourage, rare spirits of the crust would have difficulty capturing their presence. That is why they were able to enter the house and observe some spiritual movement without being foreseen.

Two repugnant figures of the disembodied chattered in a corner of a room, then retreated. The party went to the bedroom of the couple. The sight of a deformed, almost animalized being, evidencing a great mental disturbance, surprised them. It kept itself pressed close to the wall, as if hiding from someone or something.

FLÊNAI APPROACHED AND placed his right hand on the forehead of the disturbed entity, gathering his thoughts to identify the core.

Suddenly, a stark contraction in the clear and faint features of Flênai indicated that he had accessed a tragic record. Marcellus, entering into deep concentration, channeled into his mind the observations of their noble visitor. The deformed Spirit remained totally alienated, oblivious to the search they were conducting on him.

Fenai clarified, "Poor brother, he died as a mental weakling abandoned in a strong cell, where the bricklayer, Jeziel, in his previous life, was charged with the responsibility of guarding him as a jailer. As the victim did not forgive his executioner both became linked by creating strong ties that bind those who owe. In addition, for him it seems as if time stopped, for he still believes he is in that strong cell, awaiting the treatment of the jailer. The weakness that characterized him in life still typifies him after death. Any change would depend on an action of self or of some higher brother to support it. In this region of heaviness, most do not bother to intervene on behalf of others."

Taking a brief pause, he resumed, "As unconscious as he is, he could not be responsible for the phenomena that occur here. He simply inhabits the house as an extension of the cell. He does not even contemplate thoughts of revenge."

"That is why he deserves our help. How can we give you a lair? I understand that Alpha l does not deal with this kind of problem," Lunk said.

"Yes, our city fulfills tasks of another line of action. However, whenever necessary, we turn to brothers who work in life-saving tasks," said Marcellus. "We know several Spiritist centers in the crust that have workers of precious goodwill." With this information, the leader of Alpha I went into deep mental concentration. Lunk, acknowledging his efforts, lifted his hand toward Marcellus's luminous forehead, tripling the power of outreach. The transmission was made, and in a few moments, a small group entered the house - a radiant aboriginal, a burly aboriginal, and a humble old black.

Belonging to a certain spiritual caste, though great contributors to the Good, they were not yet on a vibratory level sufficiently high enough to detect the presence of Marcellus' entourage.

Lunk immediately asked Gregory, "Materialize yourself to the contact with our dear friends who have come to our aid, while we others will donate the necessary energy resources."

In a few moments, an ectoplasmic layer covered Gregory, who could then be seen by the newcomers.

The aborigenal, in a noble attitude, upon glimpsing the exalted figure of the inhabitant of Alpha 1 knelt, said, "Lord, we have received the call," and with the humility of all who awaken to the necessity of spiritual evolution, added, "We are at your service."

Gregory quickly made her stand up, as he was one who absolutely did not want to be made to look superior. "What is your name, sister?"

"Jupira, sir." And gently the girl made introductions. "These are friends who accompany me on the mission." The two companions nodded respectfully, and Jupira softly inquired, "How can we be of any service to you?"

Gregory pointed toward the poor spirit in the corner of the wall and explained the problem, requesting the action of the newcomers in favor of aiding the sufferer.

Aboriginal approached the shrunken brother and, totally influenced by Gregory, spoke and soothed the alienated soul. Under the awe of being before such a dear figure, the poor man set out to leave the house in search of a new course for his existence.

The three spiritual servicemen then retreated to support that debilitated being. They would take him to a nearby Spiritist center, where he would finally rest and receive the clarification and guidance he needed, and his destiny would now be different.

After the encounter, they undid the ectoplasmic mantle that Gregory had utilized, and the group's attention returned to the house itself. They switched to another room, a narrow one with a sofa and a bed which had suffered smoke from the combustion attacks, and which had served as a dormitory for the children. Here, they saw a young girl incarnated.

"This is Laura," Gregory pointed out. "She is the one who gives the energy to the unfortunates who attack the house. Her disagreement with her father, the revolt of a poor girl oppressed by the characteristics of her personality, makes her able to provide special order material that is used in the demonstrations. Every Poltergeist phenomenon has an incarnated donor who, as has been revealed in studies, is usually a repressed adolescent. So, this is a very typical case."

It was now late, and Laura's mother came home from work, teasing the dogs, which clearly displeased the young girl. Seeing her daughter lying on the couch and not having her dinner ready, the mother screamed at the girl who soon manufactured a reddish-orange emanation around her head.

Closely tied to the spiritual evildoers who acted in the house, though unconsciously, the emanation soon attracted them.

Marcellus's entourage witnessed the entrance of three bizarre figures of disheveled air, smelling of alcohol and nauseating presence. One of them, possibly the leader, shouted at the other, "You fool! Get it! What are you waiting for? May I fill you with a slap!"

To the surprise of Lunk and Flennai, the aforementioned collected the reddish emanations, so dense, that under the sight of the spirits, they almost covered his face. The three of them retreated hastily.

Marcellus's entourage followed them, completely imperceptible to evildoers, who were far removed from the vibratory pattern of these higher spirits.

Outside the house, there was no difficulty in finding stones and boulders. The three unfortunates crouched down to the floor, while the entourage approached to identify the actions of the evildoers.

"Get the bigger one!" shouted the leader.

And soon, a stone, weighing more than two kilos, was surrounded by the energy mass stolen from Laura.

In performing this action, the stone, enveloped in the psi material donated by the young lady, disappeared from the physical plane, or tri-dimensional, becoming a reddish ball perceptible only on the spiritual plane, or four-dimensional.

Carrying the precious package with great care, the trio burst out laughing, staring back at the house.

"I'm going to shoot," ordered the boss, demanding the rights of the attack.

They entered together - the trio with the enveloped stone and the entourage in observation. They headed for the kitchen where, from the top of the ceiling, they disentangled themselves from the wrap. The tremendous stone fell onto the ceramic floor, causing panic in the mistress of the house.

Astonished, she continued to observe more chaos as the energy that served to transport the projectiles was not exhausted at all. By the induction of the leader, the joke continued - the three, at ground level, wrapped the stone again and again, moving it here and there, before the eyes of Dona Ana Maria, until she disappeared.

With special skill, the leader of the unfortunates took the stone and, at a height of about a meter from the ground, untied the weight of the wrapper, hurling it against the kitchen cabinet. Shrapnel flew everywhere, adding to the loss some of the few cups that had still resisted the attacks.

Desperate, Dona Ana Maria ran, seeking help throughout the neighborhood. One neighbor rushed to the telephone at the nearby bar to inform the IBPP team that the attacks had resumed.

Faced with the tumult, Marcellus added, "Tomorrow, the researchers will be here, and this is important, because some friends of the family have already asked for help from a Spiritist center that has been working to capture the evildoers. Everything happens in its time. Now the researchers will have the opportunity to register with the greatest effort the evidences of these occurrences.

Soon peace will reign in this home, but the data of the phenomenon will remain forever in the archives and in the handbooks that the IBPP will leave at the disposal of those who seek the scientific face of paranormal phenomena."

Chapter XII
Reincarnation and Xenoglossia

———

THE SHIP PROCEEDED out of the South American continent, progressing over the sea, under the careful inspection of the travelers.

Marcellus broke the silence. "I recall a great philosopher who lived on Earth under the name of Schopenhauer, who said that 'if an Oriental asked me for a definition of a Westerner, I would be forced to say that he is the one who has the extravagant illusion that the birth of man is the beginning and that he was created for NOTHING.'"

"Ah, yes?" Lunk questioned with interest. "This means that at least part of the globe -the east, as I understand it – has views that are closer to reality."

"Yes, no doubt! The principle of reincarnation is central to all ancient religions and Eastern philosophies, such as Hinduism, Buddhism, Jainism, Brahmanism, etc., which favor the solid formation of the principles that have survived over time."

"And how does man, in general, understand reincarnation?" asked Flênai.

"The religions I cited - which have branched out into hundreds of others over time - and the more spiritual religions of the West, accept this fact as something necessary for the evolution of the spirit."

Gregory clarified, "This is true in regard to philosophy or religion; however, we have been struggling in our efforts to make official science accept such evidence, since we have on Earth some of our researchers with the specific mission of proving, rationally and scientifically, the existence of reincarnation."

A spark of radiance flickered across the face of Flênai, encouraging Gregory to continue. "The head of the research institute we just visited is one of the top three researchers on this subject today. The other two are Professor Hemendra Banerjee, of India and Ian Stevenson, from America. All have worked, over decades, documenting hundreds of cases - many of them with irrefutable evidence demonstrating reincarnation."

Ian Stevenson

Hemendra Nath Banerjee

HERMUS CONTRIBUTED with a brief history. "The first investigations were attempted by a process known as age regression. About a century ago, two researchers began research, and in 1911, the Frenchman De Rochas published the book *Successive Lives*. Similarly, the Italian Innocenzo Calderone launched, shortly after, the book The *Reincarnazione, Inchiesta Internazionale* known in English as *Reincarnation: An International Inquiry*. In 1946, George Browell, an American, used other media to publicize his works. He published interesting articles on the subject in the Sunday Express newspaper."

After pausing briefly, he added, "Many others have been dedicating themselves to the subject and collaborating with us. However, for our purposes today, we focus our attention specifically on the three representatives of Alpha I, of whom we spoke just now."

Marcellus, noting the others' interest in the subject, proposed, "I think it would be important for our visitors to get to know the work of one of these brothers who works on behalf of our station. Perhaps, a trip through India would demonstrate the fascinating work of our Banerjee."

Hermus, who often missed his human side, rejoiced at the suggestion, adding, "Ah yes! In the early decades of this twentieth century, systematic research on reincarnation began in India, based on the accounts of children who, from a very early age, claimed to have lived in an earlier incarnation in the form of another personality.

Such statements are taken seriously there because reincarnationist doctrines are widespread in the East. Thus, children are not inhibited in their statements. On the contrary, they are encouraged to give more details, revealing the names of places and relatives related to their previous existence."

"Unfortunately," Gregory said, "in the West, because of the predominance of another religious line and a lack of adequate information, parents interpret their children's statements as the product of the child's imagination, which inhibits these disclosures early on."

"Through research," Marcellus said, "scientists have recorded that remembrances tend to begin in early childhood, with a peak between two and four years of age, decreasing by ages seven or eight, although some individuals retain memory of the facts for a lifetime; however, that is quite rare.

The brother we will visit, Professor Hemendra Banerjee, has studied more than 700 cases of reincarnation to date - many of them published in dissertations with full scientific rigor, containing detailed accounts of the facts recorded."

Lunk asked for more details. "Tell us about this researcher."

"Our Banerjee is, in this incarnation, a respected professor at the University of Rajasthan in Jaipur, India. He has traveled throughout many countries, not only sharing his ideas but, above all, researching. He was recently in Brazil, meeting with several parapsychologists at the IBPP, where he learned of the curious case of reincarnation that the team is currently investigating."

"What kind of data did you collect that shows that this is a case of reincarnation?"

"Data was provided and supported by numerous witnesses who have reported interesting peculiarities. This is known as the case of little Simone. The facts were brought to the Institute through a family friend who knows that the girl has been speaking, for two years of age, about people and places she had never met. Very interested, the entire team went to the girl's residence.

What has attracted a lot of attention to this case is that the girl reveals evidence of a previous life with the strong support of XENOGLOSSIA.

This is the name given to the phenomenon in which a person speaks a foreign language without ever having been taught. A lot of information pertinent to the case of Simone has been compiled, and we hope it will soon be published in the form of a dissertation."

He paused briefly and continued, "The team has already collected data such as interviews with the parents and grandmother, with the girl herself, and contacts with other relatives, neighbors, and Simone's childhood friends, etc.

The data collected highlights that the girl, from infancy, showed a strange dread of airplanes. After she learned to speak Portuguese, she would occasionally insert words into her vocabulary in Italian, even though nobody in the family speaks that language - not even descendants.

Many times, Simone made references to the "other mother" or "the husband of the friend who took care of her when her mother died" - giving names and citing places, such as "the mother had died on the Capitol." The girl's grandmother kept a diary and recorded countless strange words, which, after confirmation, were found to be words in Italian. For example, Simone uttered the words spancagliaia, lusca, pane, mammina, rocanini, etc. One day, the family maid yelled at her, 'But nobody here speaks Italian' and the girl replied, 'I'll tell you.' Equally strong are the girl's accounts of "US soldiers," "bombs," "airplanes," the type of uniforms worn, ambulatories, etc., all leading the researchers to believe that the girl had previously disincarnated in Italy during the second World War. The amount of data collected leads to the conclusion that Simone had been known as Angelina in her last existence on Earth. For this to be confirmed, the researchers made attempts to verify the information "in loco", that is, in Italy - a job that requires both effort and dedication. However, the satisfaction of proving a case as curious as this, provides in itself an invaluable return."

"Very interesting, no doubt! Considering that XENOGLOSSY occurs, it is very evident that this is an indisputable case of reincarnation," confirmed Flê-nai.

"This is one of the evidences that can be considered, although there are other factors that may also suggest that such a person, today known as 'X' was once 'Y'. Once the records have been verified, the researchers will take care of the disclosure.

Outside of Brazil, one of our collaborators who is most active in disseminating the reincarnation theme is Dr. Ian Stevenson, who, with his scientific caution and rigorous methods, combined with the quality of the selected cases, has been gaining respect and credit. Because of these facts, he has published, through editors and newspapers that are traditionally demanding in regard to scientific truth, in journals such as the American Journal of Psychiatry, the Journal of the American Society for Psychical Research, the Journal of the American Medical Association, etc."

Smiling, Marcellus addressed Gregory, "Undoubtedly, the team that acknowledges the accomplishments of Alpha I is very active. We all know that our Gregory, in charge of the Communications Department, has fixed teams implanted on the planet, through which precious information is unleashed. I would also like to inform you that it is under the responsibility of our dear friend that the work of Glaucius's sector, that is to say, ecological affairs, is disseminated. In accordance with the advance plans from Gregory, it should not be long before the whole earth becomes very united in the defense of nature. It is the force of communication."

Chapter XIII
In Jaipur

———

IN A FEW MOMENTS, THE ship had crossed the Atlantic, north of Africa, and was now entering Asia on its way to India. They crossed over some extremely populated cities, which surprised Flênai. "I notice that this region is more densely populated, but the vibrating mass is not as heavy as the one we felt in the city of São Paulo, which we just left."

Marcellus explained, "Both observations are correct. Although the population of India is, numerically, much greater, it still breathes the air of peace. Well-being vibrates in the atmosphere. This is because the life of the Indians is totally governed by their religious principles. Here, abortion is condemned, and the acceptance of numerous offspring is considered a divine blessing. Those in India see themselves as servants of the "Most High", inasmuch as they serve as channelers for other brethren of the spiritual sphere to incarnate on Earth. In addition, because they have to share so many resources, they own very little in terms of material possessions. Religious doctrine teaches them that life is transitory and that material goods exist to be UTILIZED and not to be ACCUMULATED."

Lunk, with an air of approval, assessed, "The philosophy of the Indians is very interesting."

"In truth," said Marcellus, "the philosophy has deep roots in the very ancient Hindu texts dating back to 1,500 BC, called the Vedas, which cited reincarnation as an obligatory means of perfecting the soul in successive lives. These ideas survived over time, and by believing in these natural laws, the Indians went in the opposite direction of those in nations that followed the concept of materialism, which today constitutes the greatest threat to the planet. That is why the local vibrations are so much lighter here."

Flênai, realizing that the ship had parked, inquired, "In this region, could we go down without the guards?"

Marcellus asked the pilot, "Andreye, give us the position of the vibrations of the crust, please."

The pilot consulted the dashboard and typed onto the on-board computer's keyboard, receiving an immediate response which he read. "Vibrations rarefied, percentage of 2T over 25. Jaipur site, reference 3 meters above ground, lord."

"Great!" celebrated Marcellus. "We can disembark without the protective equipment."

There was approval in the countenance of Flênai and Lunk, who at last felt the lightness of the earthly air made possible by the views of the world seen and felt by these suffering people, who from the pool of their misery remind us of the symbol of their own philosophy - the lotus flower.

Although Marcellus was delighting in the happiness of acknowledging this point of light on the Earth, Hermus thought how sad it was to admit the usual necessity of protection whenever they visited the Earth and the few regions where Man did not have to fear Man himself.

When they touched the ground, Flênai stopped in front of the old building of the University of Rajasthan, completely absorbed. His companion, Lunk, accessed his mind, and they shared deep thoughts with the other.

Marcellus, not wanting to invade the privacy of the illustrious visitors, took the lead in search of Professor Banerjee, while the rest of the group remained in the gardens. Having visited his reincarnated friend numerous times, the leader of Alpha Station knew exactly where the teacher worked.

Arriving at his room, he found it empty of a physical presence. Only a disembodied brother of high moral character occupied the room. Upon the arrival of the eminent leader, the entity immediately sent him respectful compliments. "Sir! What a pleasant surprise to see you on our study sites! Can I be of any use to you?"

Marcellus, declining with reverence, inquired, "Rajay, I come in search of your protégé, Professor Hemendra Banerjee. I thought I might find him her."

With a sweet smile, as if revealing good news, Rajay explained, "Our brother traveled to Europe yesterday. He was invited, with honors, to participate in the Fifth International Congress of Psychosomatic Medicine and Hypnosis. He will be the first exhibitor, opening the event. We are doing our job, sir."

Marcellus smiled and confirmed, "For this reason, we entrusted our Banerjee to your hands! And to Gutara, too! Where is our sister?"

"She accompanied our speaker to Europe. It will provide the necessary vibrational coverage so that our representative will do well in the lectures he gives, while I stayed here to save our space."

"Great! Tell me, where will the Congress take place?"

"In the city of Mainz, at the University of Gutenberg, West Germany, sir."

Marcellus accepted this information and, with gratitude, withdrew. When he returned to his entourage, he clarified the location of the professor and provided his favorable opinion on making the trip to Europe, seeking the opportunity to see and hear Banerjee as he disseminated his work.

With the agreement of all, the ship headed northward. With sonic speed, the distance that connected the two geographical points passed quickly. Soon the ship was flying over Europe, and Marcellus instructed the pilot, "Andreye, find the University of Gutenberg on the electronic map, please."

With skill, the ship's commander typed the name of the location onto the panel, and a sequence of images appeared on the video monitor, indicating the route to be followed. Andreye transferred the commands to the thermosensitive control and waited for the ship to approach the location.

In a few seconds, he parked the ship.

"Give us the local time, Andreye."

"It's 6 hours, 34 minutes and 27 seconds, sir."

"Connect the spectrographic probe to the University and locate the auditorium."

The travelers remained attentive to the image capture panel, while the pilot swept the various rooms of the building with the probe. "Here, sir."

"Well, it's just dawn. Let's look for our Banerjee at some nearby hotel."

Hermus, attempting to collaborate, suggested, "We can use the data transfer. Give me the sensitive device, Andreye. I will try to transmit the image."

The pilot handed the biologist a small box resembling a camera. Hermus, placing it at the level of his forehead, closed his eyes and went into deep concentration. At the end of the operation, he pressed the small button of the device, which expelled an image, similar to a photograph, printed on a film.

Marcellus looked at him and smiled. "Uh ... your thinking reproduced our teacher, reasonably," and handing the film to the pilot, ordered, "Put it on the decoder, Andreye."

The pilot took the "photo-thought" and introduced it to the panel. Automatically, the screen emitted an overview of the city and swept from person to person, with incredible speed, until a specific image was caught. It had located Banerjee, who was still asleep.

Identifying the location, they traveled there. During the course, Marcellus asked his pilot to use the probe to check the general state of the one they would visit.

Andreye, using the ship's advanced equipment, interpreted, "Harmonious physical state. Only exhaustion of the nervous system, at the level of 12%. Good thinking, 1 by 8, state of relaxation. We catch small tension in the muscles near the spine, which will cause a slight headache upon awakening."

The ship was parked, and everyone got ready to go down, protected, this time, by the guards.

Chapter XIV
New Directions

———

IN THE HOTEL ROOM, the professor's physical body rested, while the flowing silver cord extending from the back of his head indicated his spirit was elsewhere.

Marcellus approached the bed and rubbed his right hand gently across the thymus gland of Banerjee. Although earthly medicine does not appreciate the inherent value of it, the high spiritual plane defines the gland as the point of equilibrium - that is, through it, one can evaluate the state of harmony of the organic whole.

"Hermus, do you know how old our brother on Earth is today?" asked the leader, referring to Professor Banerjee.

"Well, he left Alpha I in 1928, having come to light on Earth in 1929. Today he is 41 years old."

"Do you have reports of his life programming?"

"Yes, this issue was discussed by our bioengineering experts recently at a meeting I attended. Our Banerjee had their MOB-Biological Organizer Template planned to give life to his earthy body for 46 or 47 years. However, due to the lack of another who can help in the ways Banerjee has, the higher plane prayed to him to lengthen his stay. So, he will be incarnated for at least another ten years. According to the new plan, he will be discharged around 1986, without any physical suffering - simply the blockage of an artery, which will cause a rapid heart attack."

"Proper foresight. He has been doing great work, and the planet needs it here."

In a moment, the teacher's spirit returned to engage the body and awaken. It was accompanied by a beautiful spiritual entity in golden. Surprised by the presence of the visitors, Gutara knelt at Marcellus's feet, begging for his blessing.

"Master!"

The leader of Alpha I raised her affectionately, causing her to modestly dismiss the deference.

Gutara jubilantly proclaimed, "We have just returned from Alpha I. My protégé currently attends level 5-B from the group of scientists incarnated."

Marcellus smiled at the news and introduced the beautiful girl. "This is Gutara. When Banerjee was reincarnated, she was appointed to be his mentor here." Hugging her in a fatherly way, he complimented, "This was a very correct decision, since you have seen the impeccable path followed by our teacher!"

Lowering her eyes, damp from the gratitude for her acknowledged work, Gutara approached her protege. She knew that Banerjee, even in his incarnate condition, freed from the physical body by sleep, did not exactly make out the entourage. The mentor lightly touched the professor's forehead to magnify the faculties of his vision, and suddenly he could identify Marcellus, the friend he had not seen for many years, since on his frequent visits to Alpha the leader rarely made himself felt.

Homesick and moved by his presence, Banerjee embraced him, and with an embarrassed, yet humble voice, uttered, "Ah, my dear brother, how I have suffered on this material plane...how much suffering rages on this earth. I devote myself as much as I can for our purposes, but I do not know if I accomplish my tasks as expected."

Marcellus embraced him with tenderness, responding, "We are immensely proud of you! So much so that today we bring two friends interested in getting to know you, as well as the work to which you dedicate yourself with special effort."

Gutara widened the professor's perspective even further, allowing him to envision the contours of Lunk and Flênai. The professor stopped, realizing that they were not beings of earthly evolution.

Confused, he tried in vain to analyze what was going on. Stunned, he could no longer identify where he was. Gutara, realizing the uneasiness of the excessive enlargement of his visual capacity, hastened to put him back into his physical body, acknowledging that he required time to awaken.

- Lunk asked the mentor, "When he wakes up, will he remember seeing us?"

"Certainly not. First, his vision was swift, not allowing him time to fix any details. Second, the human brain has no possibility of recording what has no comparative elements."

Little by little, the professor resumed consciousness and opened his eyes. In the room, he felt somewhat euphoric, a mixture of sensations he had never experienced. He had a flash of memory that he had dreamed of an old friend, but he could not remember his face. "Oh, how silly! It was just a dream," he said with a laugh. He noted that the clock indicated the hour to awaken, and he jumped out of bed.

While Banerjee, oblivious to the entourage of friends present, performed the ritual of morning hygiene, the group continued their conversation. "Gutara, what will your guardianship say at today's congress?" Gregory asked.

"Initially, he will talk about the theme of REINCARNATION, A SCIENTIFIC REALITY, and then he will provide an example with the curious case of the boy named Gopal."

"And what kind of audience will he have?"

"I know that researchers from all over the world have been invited. Of course, among them, we will have the ACCESSIBLE ones who, in the face of irrefutable evidences, will adhere to the idea, and the INACCESSIBLES, who are already predisposed to deny any evidence. The skeptics will be the problem as always," informed Gutara with a smile.

With a laugh, Gregory recalled the case of Flammarion, who one day, in a session of the Academy of Science, shared a hilarious story.

"The physicist, Dr. Du Moncel, presented Edison's phonograph to the learned assembly. After the presentation, the apparatus was put down to play the phrase recorded on its respective cylinder. There was, then, a middle-aged scholar of the mind, a perfect representative of the traditions of classical culture, nobly revolting against audacity. Of the innovator, he rushed over to Du Moncel, and grabbing him by the neck, shouted, "Miserable! We will not be deceived by a ventriloquist!"

This was on March 11, 1878. What is even more puzzling is that, six months later, on September 30, in a similar session, the aggressor was very pleased to state that, after a thorough examination, he had found nothing more in the case than simple ventriloquism, even though one cannot admit that a vile metal can replace the noble apparatus of human phonation! According to this scholar, the phonograph was nothing more than an illusion of acoustics."

Everyone laughed, and the conversation continued until the professor, somewhat tense and with a slight headache, left the room.

At that moment, the visitors of Aldebaran mentally colluded, and Flênai stated, "It would be interesting to know the other scientists who will be present at this Congress. We were called to come from our distant constellation in order to bring a solution. We have something in mind. For this, we need to initiate contacts with the incarnated scientific community, and we realize that this is the ideal opportunity."

Marcellus, exultant at the news, proposed that they should go immediately to the auditorium and later locate Gutara and the professor.

Because the distance between the hotel and the University was minimal, they chose to use their ability to fly. While transporting, Lunk and Flênai remained in communion of thought, since a visual ring of light united both mental domes.

Hermus, intrigued, wondered to himself what the reason was for that ring. What were they planning? However, no clue occurred to him.

The entourage arrived at the entrance to the auditorium where the Congress would convene. Marcellus, fixing upon the first incoming Congressmen, considered his decision to reincarnate and realized that, in thirty years or so, he would be a colleague of those who did not even notice him now. He thought to himself, "I will find many of these brethren - even though they will be far older than I - when I am again in the bonds of the flesh."

Suddenly his countenance appeared grayish, revealing his grief, but he concentrated on the importance of such an experience, and the gray quickly became transmuted into radiant silver light.

Flênai, who had captured his thoughts, stated, "You will not reincarnate on Earth. We have another proposal, a much stronger solution. We believe that, if we can count on some of those congressmen we know today, instead of going down to Earth, as soon as all of us together have implemented our project, we will go up to Aldebaran. You will come with us. This is a very deserved promotion."

Marcellus, confused by the happiness of this proposal to help solve the Earth's problem and the embarrassment of leaving his post and responsibilities in Alpha I, remained fixed, rehearsing a smile.

Lunk, probing him, asserted, "Marcellus, you've done your job. You've driven that star station for over two hundred and fifty years. You have fought for the scientific progress of the planet and brought to it, through your apprentices, what is most advanced in terms of technology. When Divine Goodness directed you towards the pursuit of our aid in Aldebaran, the doors to individual ascension were already open to you. The goal of all Spirits, whether those of earthly evolution, like you, or those of any star in the universe, will always be progress. This is the law. When we first came into contact with Alpha I, a new era began in its history, just as it did for Earth. It is time to turn the direction of the study station over to the hands of another Spirit. In addition, you, for the merits you have won, will follow us towards evolution, which has little scope here in which to expand."

Marcellus closed his eyes, and raising his mind to the Most High, recognized that his efforts of two hundred and fifty years were worth much more than those few unforgettable seconds. Lowering his forehead, he confirmed, "Yes, yes, I will go to Aldebaran if that is my Creator's desire. I AM to serve you."

Marcellus

GREGORY AND HERMUS happily embraced their great leader, and everyone marveled that the luminous ring, which had previously united only Flênai and Lunk, now also embraced the mental dome of Marcellus.

At the entrance to the auditorium, the committee analyzed the approaching congressmen. Most of them were accompanied by high entities, which denoted the evolutionary level of these incarnates.

"Many of them come from our city," Gregory explained to the visitors of Aldebaran. And turning to Hermus, he pointed, "Look who's coming."

Everyone smiled as they reviewed the colleague who now inhabits the planet under the name of George Meek.

Marcellus explained, "This is a great friend. Born in the United States, he graduated as an engineer and comes from our star. He came to Earth with the mission of researching and disseminating paranormal phenomena, and he does it with determination. That is why you are here today. Our dear Meek tries to always be aware of all research within the theme that it is his responsibility to develop on Earth."

George Meek

LUNK AND FLÊNAI FIXED it with a very special interest. They seemed to delve into their past, present, and future.

"Here is Friedrich Juergenson. Good to see him here! He is the one who first recorded the voice phenomenon known as EVP - Electronic Voice Phenomenon - more than ten years ago. Thanks to this innovation introduced by him, several societies or listening posts have been created on Earth, in different parts of the planet, to register voices in recorders," said Gregory.

"Who are those who accompany the Engineer Meek?" asked Lunk.

"Ah yes, to his right are Hans Heckman. To the left is his great and constant research companion, the German engineer Ernst Senkowski, born in this city."

"And he who follows immediately behind? Who is he?" inquired Lunk.

"That's William John O'Neil, an electronics technician who worked until recently for the US government, but he's not part of Meek's group."

"But he will be," Lunk prophesied with a smile, to which Flênai remarked, "In fact, it serves our interests."

To everyone's surprise, Flênai asked to leave the group for a moment and went to stand beside the American Meek. With his flat right hand, he probed Meek's thoughts. Lunk did the same with O'Neil, who had sat down. The two representatives of Aldebaran created a link between the minds of both scientists, generating such a strong feeling of mutual cooperation that the reaction was immediate. O'Neil turned around, giving Meek an acknowledging eye. Unimpressed by coincidence, they smirked in embarrassment with a nod.

Lunk and Flênai returned with expressions of happiness on their faces.

Hermus, intrigued questioned mentally: - "Why they have focused only on Meek and O'Neil?"

These thoughts were cut short by the arrival of Banerjee, accompanied by Gutara. Alpha I's entourage would be willing to accompany him as well, to which Lunk stopped: a couple also entered the auditorium.

Perceiving his interest, Marcellus clarified, "He's an EVP researcher named Harsh-Fischback, and his lady is quite supportive."

"But he is an excellent medium," said Lunk, "who has a mediumistic capacity that interests us greatly!"

Flênai approached the woman and, probing her mind, widened his perception. Suddenly Harsh-Fischbach's wife felt enveloped in candor, something inexplicably good. Lunk concentrated on the top of the woman's head, depositing a golden circle that he manipulated properly.

Hermus watched closely, questioning the meaning of all that.

His curiosity went unanswered, and he followed behind the entourage who was about to accompany Banerjee. Soon, the professor would rise to the podium, carrying the results of hard work, according to his mission that had been established in the station.

Chapter XV
The Gopal Case

WITH THE GREETINGS and introductions completed, Banerjee was called up to the podium, as the first speaker, before the respectable and attentive audience. Gutara stood beside the teacher, and with her right hand placed upon his dome, established a strong energetic link between his mind and hers, emitting a continuous stream of crystalline energy, evidenced by his sudden eloquence and firmness, not characteristic of the modest and discreet Banerjee.

He began, "I know that many have never thought that the human personality transcends the physical body, that is, that part of the whole that makes up Man survives the death of his physical body.

To reach this conclusion, I have embarked on meticulous research, and I conclude today that reincarnation is a phenomenon that can be proven by facts. To guarantee the authenticity of such research, I even considered the possibility of fraud.

However, after more than seven hundred cases studied in the light of rigorous scientific methods, I have concluded that reincarnation is more than simply a possibility - it is a reality.

Certain religions - Islam, Christianity, etc. - deny that reincarnation exists, because according to their doctrines, after earthly life ends, the whole creation will wait for the Day of Final Judgment - when some will have claimed the joys of the heavens and others will be condemned to the fires of hell. I deduce that this is not even coherent!

Today, in order to rehabilitate the image of religion, scientific methods of investigation must be employed rather than traditional metaphysical arguments. What penetrates the heart has to be confirmed by intelligence.

That was the path I chose to tread. Recording evidence of the reality of reincarnation, I sought to find a scientific basis for it, for without a disciplined exploration, any philosophical principle loses its validity in the face of science, and without a new vision, civilization rests solely on materialism.

According to the view of the materialists, everything in the universe falls within the physical principles of time, space, mass and causality, leaving no room for the spiritual element. However, my research confirms that there is something that transcends the jurisdiction of today's physics. Allow me to provide an example by way of a story."

Banerjee paused, and, immersed in the deep silence of the attentive audience, resumed his words under the positive influence of Gutara.

"The research that I call "THE GOPAL CASE" refers to a boy in Delhi, India, born by that name, in 1956.

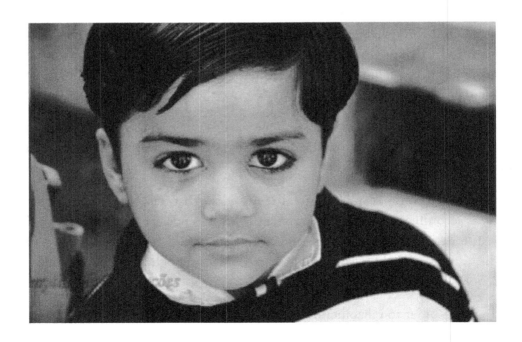

Gopal, born in 1956, in New Delhi, India

WHEN HE WAS BETWEEN two and three years of age, his family tried to teach him the name of his father, Mr. Gupta. The boy would contest, informing them that his father's name was Sharma. They encouraged him to provide more information, and the boy reported, quite naturally, that he had three brothers and that one of them had killed him.

Intrigued by the strange statements, Mr. Gupta began to question Gopal in a normal, casual way."

"And where did you live with your father and brothers?"

"In Mathura."

"And what did you do there?"

"I had a store called Sukh Sancharak."

Perplexed by the staunchness of the statements, Mr. Gupta was surprised to learn, while conversing with friends, that a tragedy had occurred, years before, in a nearby town, called Mathura, where a brother had shot the owner of a pharmacy, Mr. Shaktipal Sharma.

More perplexed still, Mr. Gupta went to that city, trying to locate members of the Sharma family. At that time, our research center at Jaipur University became aware of the case and began to participate and guide the search for evidence.

We accompanied Mr. Gupta to Mathura, and there we located the widow of Shaktipal. Upon learning of the existence of a boy who claimed to have been her ex-husband, the widow wished to meet him.

It struck everyone with surprise that when the boy, Gopal, spotted the woman, his wife in a previous life, he not only recognized her immediately, but also denounced her, with embarrassment and regret, in an accusing tone."

"When I asked you for the 5,000 rupees, you refused to give them to me, telling me to take the value from the pharmacy. As I went there, my little brother killed me with a shot!"

The widow, astonished, confirmed the validity of that occurrence.

A few days later, we led the boy, Gopal, to Mathura, and he was asked to try to locate his old address. Gopal immediately stood at the head of our group as we traveled through the streets of the city. Finally, he stopped and pointed at a residence, stating, "This is my house. I lived upstairs."

He later located his pharmacy and gave precise details about the scene of the crime, like the position of the body, place hit by the bullet etc.

Another piece of corroborating evidence was achieved when he was given, in his hands, a Sharma family album, and Gopal (Shaktipal) was able to identify several relatives."

"All the facts here are documented in a study consisting of more than 200 pages," At that moment, Banerjee took into his hands the dossier, placing it on the platform before him and continued, "with the support of 18 witnesses, complete with photos and films, available to researchers."

Before the teacher finished the first part of his presentation, Marcellus's entourage waved to Gutara, acknowledging her for the performance of her tutelage.

Surely, many of the researchers, scientists and scholars present there, in support of the impeccable reputation of Professor Banerjee, would come to think about this reality - reincarnation. This was another seed planted for the harvest of the dedicated Indian teacher, whose harvest will be enjoyed when he returns to his true homeland - Alpha I.

Chapter XVI
A Proposal

———

DURING THE INTERMISSION, many of the congressmen retreated to the entrance hall for coffee, discussing with enthusiasm the subject shared by Professor Banerjee.

Lunk and Flênai saw this as the first opportunity to coordinate some direct interference with the terrestrials.

Flênai approached George Meek and mentally suggested a desire for coffee. In response, the American engineer suddenly invited his companion, Dr. Heckman, to join him in the hall, while Lunk, stationed near O'Neil, initiated the same idea. As the three men approached the same location, the meeting of the three was inevitable. As they converged, O'Neil commented, "You look familiar."

"I'm George Meek. I came from Franklin, North Carolina in the United States."

"Ah, we already have something in common. I am also American. Nice to meet you. I'm William O'Neil."

"Ah, this is my colleague, Dr. Hans Heckman."

"Greetings!"

Lunk smiled at Marcellus and prophesied, "This friendship will last for decades in our favor."

The leader of Alpha I, capturing this much sought-after collaboration on behalf of planet Earth, focused attention on the conversation of the three incarnate researchers, while Lunk retreated to the auditorium again.

"You are a researcher of ...?" began O'Neill.

"EVP" Meek replied. "I've collected a lot of recordings of disincarnated voices on tape recorders."

"Oh, very interesting. I am very curious, and I admire your achievement," O'Neil said, smiling. "Since I retired from the US Navy, I have been devoting myself to electronics in paranormal research."

"Now, that's a coincidence! Just this morning, my colleagues addressed the need to join with someone who has specific expertise in this area. Would it interest you to join our studies?"

A glow illuminated O'Neil's face as he immediately accepted the proposal, and to more fully understand the field, he asked for additional clarification.

"I think these communications with the spiritual world via electronics are not new."

"Oh no, absolutely not," asserted Heckman.

"Since the beginning of the century, some attempts have been made to enable communication via devices. The first of these researchers was Thomas Edison, who tried to create an apparatus in order to contact the Superior Astral. Incidentally, even the Morse Code was used! In 1911, a German named Zelst built a device that he named Dinamistograph, and through it, he managed to communicate with his late father via Morse Code."

"It is important to emphasize that these devices have often been suggested by the spirits, which shows their great interest in promoting such communication in two ways - between there and here!"

O'Neil spoke thoughtfully, inspired by Lunk who, with both hands flat on his mental dome, made him unravel the plan of action of the enlightened brothers of Aldebaran.

"Look, if we were able to effect this communication across astral interplanes by electronic means, everyone would be led to admit the existence of the spirits, the survival of the soul after physical death... and finally, that reincarnation is an incontestable fact! In short," he said, extremely excitedly, "all spiritual ideas, proclaimed by various religions, such as Buddhism, Spiritism and so on would be proved and would cease to be philosophy and would be recognized as pure reality! The whole world would know of this achievement, via electronic devices and would not be able to refute them. Today, the media for sharing this information has been mostly mediums, and this can be quite subjective. There are those who accept them and those who do not. However, by electronic means, everything would be different! If a recorder can pick up audible and clear voices, with identification from the transmitter communicating beyond, who could refute this? Maybe we could make efforts to upgrade the devices."

O'Neil was visibly transformed. He had just assimilated the work he would develop over the next few years.

Influenced by Flênai, Meek complemented with the same level of enthusiasm. "Yes, maybe there are other ways, even better than the use of recorders!"

"Yes," Dr. Heckman said, "what if we tried radio wave communication? Of course, it is not impossible, or perhaps even television."

"Well, my knowledge of electronics tells me that this is possible," O'Neil said positively, "but we will have to work hard to discover the form of access unless we are supported by the Higher Spiritual Plane. In that case, they can guide us in the assembly of devices and so we can even get pictures via the television. We can talk in two ways through radio waves, that is, using the same radio and other devices, such as computer, telephone. Any electronic route would be an open field for access!"

Lunk, looking at Marcellus, Hermus, and Gregory, who watched the conversation with great surprise, said with a broad smile, "Impressed? Are you finding it difficult to carry out this plan? But it is exactly OUR proposal!"

Marcellus felt his eyes dampen. This solution would be much more definitive. Even the emergence of the greatest medium of all time would not be as convincing as communication via electronics! Of course, a medium could be refuted by the various religions which do not want to see their belief systems shaken. As for official science, it would not be difficult for academics to testify against a medium as being fraudulent. However, what scientist would deny an electronic device? What religion would dare to testify against such real and incontestable evidence?

Despite not understanding the methods that would be employed, Marcellus looked up at the Most High, and in his silence, gratitude was heard addressed to the Father. His prayers were heard. From the distant star of Aldebaran came the solution to realign the mental conduct of Man.

The brothers incarnate, perhaps, will record a milestone in the history of the Earth - before Lunk and Flênai and after them.

The dream of communication via voices and images

Chapter XVII
The Future

———

LUNK, WHO HAD MOVED away from the group, now returned from the interior of the auditorium, accompanying the Harsh-Fischbach couple to a small cafe in the foyer hall. Drawing on the sensitivity of Mrs. Maggy, he caused her to bump into Meek, who immediately apologized and began a dialogue.

The extension of the link was expanding from the initial three collaborators to five - all of them with the same goals.

After this brief contact, the couple retired to attend the lecture, leaving the three researchers talking like old acquaintances, under the supervision of the spiritual friends. "With Meek's enthusiasm, everything will become easy for us," said Flênai. "Now is the time to start our plan."

Flênai, laying his hands on the forehead of the lively and eloquent Meek, inspired him and the researcher suddenly asserted, "Friends, do you want to know something? To better share our accomplishments and our experiences, we need to eliminate the prejudices and limits placed on us. Beginning with taxes on the official sciences, this makes our research difficult because we are often evaluated and feared to be regarded as crazy," and, thoughtfully, added, "Let's start a society! What would we call it ... um ... METASCIENCE ... METASCIENCE ASSOCIATES?"

Showing great satisfaction with this idea shared among by the mentors, Lunk and Flênai, cheerfully fraternized. It appeared the first members of the society had just been baptized.

"Of course," O'Neil said, "with this society we will not have constraints. We will explore such matters as the etheric body, the energy fields, the parallel worlds, and we will go further, within the precious territory of inter-astral spaces."

Flênai, noting the possibility of interfering with the sensitivity of this technician in electronics, took advantage of his mediumship to complete his plans, influencing O'Neil to add,

"Through this society, we can expect change so that, with certainty, new times will arise for us on Earth! Times of peace, with Man awakening to the upper course that fits him. He will discover that his "enemy" is not another human being, but his own inferiority that he will have to overcome."

Sensitized by the grandiose prospect that "chance" had made possible, they made plans to meet together the same night, when they would draw up the first plans.

Marcellus inquired, "But, but our skillful scientists of Alpha I would not know how to overcome the barriers of the spaces, penetrating one and the other field, going from the 4th to the 3rd dimension. This is a task for which we are not prepared."

"We know this" Lunk admitted. "However, today we will send telepathic messages to Aldebaran, requesting them to send some of our masters in universal engineering. They will briefly bring in our beloved Alpha I Station and begin the training of their scientists.

Let us also avail ourselves of the interchange that Alpha I promotes at night, when it receives the researchers of the physical world for lessons and clarifications. Some incarnates will be selected to be part of this advanced group, and through them, we will lay our roots on Earth for effective exchange.

The first exceptional figure of this exchange has already been elected. The engineer, Meek, with his enthusiasm, will evoke the sequence of events.

Through the US-based Metascience Foundation, he will create the first devices, under our supervision, which will advance our services...supported, of course, by Heckman's knowledge and facilitated by O'Neil's clairvoyance and clarity, through mediumship. This trio will be the tireless support we need.

We will spread tentacles of love throughout the globe.

We believe that, within the short space of twenty-five Earth years, communication between both sides will have become a worldwide reality.

It may seem like a long time to the terrestrials, but considering that in the last eight thousand years of history no direct communication has been maintained, this time is short in order to equip ourselves.

We have in mind that everything will be done through our knowledge on Aldebaran in collaboration with the brothers of Alpha I. The terrestrials will be just the "receptive end", since the terrestrial devices are still too primitive for spatial interpenetration. It will be up to us to meet all the deficiencies in human knowledge and equipment.

Tonight, we will follow Meek's temporary unfolding during his sleep and lead him to Alpha I, where he will be instructed on the first device to be built. Our first direct communications will be made via radio waves - and the first device will be called MARK I."

Flênai smiled and said, "Because it will be the first landmark of the New Age."

With a smile of agreement, Lunk continued, "We will create as many inventions as we need. We predict that, in the 70's, we will make radio communications, which will be called Spiricom. In the 80's, we will get better enough to enter the television waves. This will be known as Vidicom. At the beginning of the 90's, we will have perfected ourselves to start the expansion."

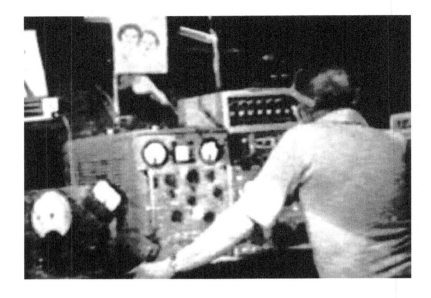

SPIRICOM - Apparatus designed by O'Neil

MARCELLUS WAS ELATED.

Lunk, spreading his right hand upward, blessed the three friends of Alpha I with golden rays. Fondly raising Marcellus, he prophesied, "As you'll see ... you will no longer have to reincarnate on Earth. We all, together, will act upon the terrestrial brothers to carry out our plan."

Flênai, smiling at Gregory, commented, "The 90s will be the beginning of the spread, and by this time, our Konstantin Raudive will already be in a position to take over the mediation. He will coordinate a broad Season - which will grow with the increase in the number of deceased who wish to mitigate the pain of longing experienced by their loved ones and who will wish to add their efforts to this cause. We will move forward using the new technical resources that will arise, thanks to the progress of computers, cell phones, Skype etc ... Transcommunication may be the most concrete way to prove that life continues after death. However, we will remain attentive. This project has to have two ways of action." He paused and continued, "We cannot act if the yearning for all of this does not come from those who inhabit the crust. In other words, the ascension of the planet is not in our hands, but in those of men. Thousands of eyes will accompany them and watch. As always."

A source of light descended from a higher dimension, showing yet again that beings of the highest hierarchy see everything. A sense of cosmic twinning penetrated the minds of Alpha's friends as the visitors became diaphanous ......and disappeared.

Everything else possible through computer science

Afterword

THIS WORK IS A VERY important expose on the inner, or other reality, of which most are not aware. The story line here is coherent, cogent and consistent with that which exists in the non physical, etheric planes, as has been given to us from the Masters and Higher Beings, in this most recent unfolding of the planet.

Moreover, the advanced level of the understandings of the science, the technology and the conceptual knowing, demonstrates the authenticity of the work and the credibility of the source – both from this channel, and otherwise.

In essence, it works as a full and comprehensive body of material enmeshed cleverly within a flowing discourse that educates, enlivens and elevates as it progresses. What is particularly impressive is how the theme of showing the reader, and thus, mankind, that there is life after the passing is used in an astute and almost scholarly manner to simultaneously filter in the other, higher information and knowledge that is so important to impart here. That is to say, the history of our planet, the relationship of our race to those of the others who, although discarnate and ancestral, have progressed far beyond the current, confused state of our humanity.

When one reaches the part with the radio transmissions and magnetic tape recordings, among other almost primitive human technologies, comparatively speaking, the illustration of the 'catchment center', instantly takes the work to a whole new level at that point. It is there, where everything that occurs on this planet is recorded and "archived in hyper-rotation holograms". With this depiction, and the statement of the reality behind it, as presented here, the reader has no place left to go, except inward and deep, to understand and accept our physical limitations, as opposed to the advanced and 'futuristic' level, if you will, of the higher, inter dimensional realms and beings shepherding the relatively spiritually ignorant, egotistic and materialistic breed of human souls.

This is reminiscent of the life between lives phases where one is shown, in similar mode, on sliding screens, scenes from their most recent incarnation, the options and possibilities, or probabilities that were then also available, and the various choices for subsequent incarnation, as we understand this to be. And this is not to mention that it is a just a handy way to describe to the unknowing the idea of Akasha, and the storehouse of records and moments in the skein of time. This, to me, was more of a revelation and a highlight of the journey through the reading of this work.

Furthermore, the illustrations and description of the Spiritual City resonates deeply, as well, as it a reminder of the clear and consistent descriptions of portions of Atlantis, as described repeatedly in numerous readings by the pre-eminent seer, Edgar Cayce. Yet, it has a character and an intelligence of design that is uniquely its own, as it should.

For the statement that it is etherealized above the land mass in Brazil, while a familiar concept to some, is an idea placed here in this work to lead the mind of the unknowing to a new vision of the non physical and its potentialities.

In this setting, again, credibility beyond mere human creation and contrivance is apparent here to the knowing eye and inner senses. As we then travel on to planet earth with the visiting group of higher beings here, it was a comfort to hear the words of trepidation and almost shock they expressed at the inhumanities we humans perpetrate as far as our brutal wars, racial discrimination, the proliferation of planetary destruction, the abuse of nuclear technology and power, deceit by governments and men, subjugation, and the sheer hypocrisy that abounds here – and all for the cause of materialism.

What provides a strong sense of vindication here, however, and cause for a deep breath of relief, for example, is the reference to Dr. Ian Stevenson and his research. I have studied his works, and those of his successors, quite extensively, and seeing this mention of him here was both heartwarming, an affirmation, and a resounding message I felt. The point being that I have been espousing this phenomenon of young children's unadulterated claims of past lives for years, and found Dr. Stevenson to be a remarkably careful researcher. He was a pioneer, indeed, and his gift of the meticulous and methodical scientific approach to this syndrome struck a knowing cord in me. Thus, I, for one, pursued it aggressively and faithfully.

Such that in oral presentations I have delivered, I have referred to his work consistently over the years, but to see it mentioned here, in this powerful piece, was a much welcomed feeling and very gratifying, given the higher sources at work in propounding this knowledge as well. It made the whole reading experience here quite worthwhile, but that is not to say that it was not otherwise so. I might also add that much of the casework of Dr. Stevenson was conducted in India!

In the Chapter, "New Directions", the contact with Professor Banjeree, both in his sleep state and at the podium, reminded me of so much of what I and others have known and have experienced in like kind, too. In the "Gopal Case", which he lectured upon here, the evidence is overwhelming and any objective reader cannot realistically doubt its veracity or import. With the intercession there of Gutara, the beautiful spiritual mentor, the whole scenario takes on a totally different flavor and anyone who has understood or experienced this combination of energies and gifts, knows exactly what is transpiring here, and how.

Finally, the conclusion, or "Proposal" now seems to be coming to light, both with the prolific work of Dr. Rinaldi, and otherwise, and it is not inadvertent that this piece would have been delivered through Her then, as indicated.

These closing words of this piece appropriately sum it all up here, and opened the door, I suspect, to what was projected then and what has, and is, indeed transpiring now:

"The '90s will be the beginning of the spread ... and by this time, our Konstantin Raudive will already be in a position to take over the mediation. He will coordinate a broad Season - which will grow with the increase in the number of deceased who wish to mitigate the pain of longing experienced by their loved ones and who will wish to add their efforts to this cause. We will move forward using the new technical resources that will arise, thanks to the progress of computers, cell phones, Skype etc.... Transcommunication may be the most concrete way to prove that life continues after death. However, we will remain attentive. This project has to have two ways of action."

He paused and continued, "We cannot act if the yearning for all of this does not come from those who inhabit the crust. In other words, the ascension of the planet is not in our hands, but in those of men. Thousands of eyes will accompany them and watch. As always..."

Consequently, it is for us, now in the human form here, to deliver these messages and all of these teachings so those who are drawn to it, may absorb it and share it, and be relieved from the terror of the unknown. In so doing, it will become one day a universal understanding that the passing is but a mere change of form, and not at all what is known to be a 'death'.

Finally, as I was reading this work, I felt I was living it. The level and the manner of delivery of the information, as it flowed effortlessly through the wording and phraseology, took me home, to places where I know it all emanates from.

I am grateful for the privilege of reading this Book, and the honor of being asked to analyze and to review it here. It is truly a most remarkable, timely and important work, that in my view needs to be heard and shared with the masses.

New York, New York - February 2020

Namaste'

Joseph Gargano

www.thespiritualaw.com

Last Words

———

THIS LIFE HAS BEEN a gift, providing me the opportunity to serve those on the Other Side since I was 18 years old.

Thanks to those friends; I have so much to thank them for.

I opened this book thanking my deceased husband, Fernando, for his daily support throughout the beginning of my journey to serve Spirituality.

I would like to close this book thanking those friends without whom I would be unable to assist the Other Side's request of publishing their story in English.

To my friend, Lisa Laniewski, who patiently edited the English version - which, I am sure, was hard work!

I especially must thank Amy Zubak - who, very modestly and anonymously, works day after day assisting me and our Spirit Friends with indescribable dedication.

We are a team - and I couldn't waste this opportunity to express my gratitude publicly.

So, initially I offered this book to Fernando and the Friends from Alpha, and I want to end it by thanking Amy, in my name and on behalf of all of our Spirit Friends, for all she does.

Sonia Rinaldi

May 2020

Made in the USA
Coppell, TX
04 November 2020

40646385R00079